# The Traveler
*Find Your Way*

Interview with WT Gillespie

The Aiki Dialogues - N. 4

The Traveler - Find Your Way
Interview with WT Gillespie

Simone Chierchini

Copyright © 2021 Simone Chierchini

First Edition

Published: Aikido Italia Network Publishing

Pentahedron Ltd, Tavanaghmore, Foxford, Co. Mayo, Ireland

(00353) 083 -87-13927

info@aikidoitalianetworkpublishing.com

www.aikidoitalianetworkpublishing.com

Front and Back Cover Photos © WT Gillespie. Reproduced with the copyright owner authorization

Cover and layout design by Simone Chierchini

Some of the images utilized in this book were found online. Despite our best efforts, we could not locate the correct copyright holder. No challenge to copyright is intended

No part of this book can be reproduced or used in any form or by any means without prior written permission of the publisher

ISBN: 9798539614379

Imprint: Independently published on Amazon KDP

Simone Chierchini

# The Traveler
*Find Your Way*

Interview with WT Gillespie

Aikido Italia Network Publishing

# Table of Contents

| | |
|---|---|
| About WT Gillespie | 7 |
| Introduction | 11 |
| California | 15 |
| Good Old Days' Stories | 23 |
| Japan | 29 |
| The Training Culture at the Aikikai Hombu Dōjō | 35 |
| Furuya Sensei's Helping Hand | 41 |
| Asa-keiko, the Morning Class | 47 |
| Balancing Life in Tokyo | 51 |
| Living with O-sensei's Legacy in Japan | 57 |
| The True Greatness of Kisshomaru Ueshiba | 63 |
| The Yin/Yang of the Grading System in Aikidō | 69 |
| Searching for Aikidō Applied | 77 |
| The Aiki-body | 89 |
| Being an Aikidō Pioneer in China | 97 |

*William Gillespie and his family*

# About WT Gillespie

William Gillespie was referred to me by a young Italian student at the *Aikikai Hombu Dōjō* who had trained recently with him in Japan. Originally from California, William has lived in East Asia since 1997: Japan, China and South Korea. He holds the rank of 6th *dan* in *Aikikai Aikidō* and is a student of the Aikikai Hombu Dōjō in Tokyo and currently one of the senior foreign students there. William is the founder of Beijing Aikikai and the China-based group of Aikikai *dōjō* known as CAikikai, which has dōjō in five cities in mainland China.

A graduate of the University of California, Los Angeles and Loyola Law School, William started Aikidō formally in 1987 in a traditional dōjō in "Little Tokyo" in Los Angeles under Reverend Kensho Furuya - who stressed the martial roots of Aikidō as indispensable to the full benefit of training. Furuya *sensei* lived in Hombu Dōjō in 1969, as *kenshusei* under Kisshomaru Ueshiba *Doshu*. From 1970 to 1972, Furuya sensei studied under Mitsunari Kanai *shihan*, a student of O-*sensei* and founder of New England Aikikai, while completing his Masters Degree in Japanese studies and East Asian Religions at Harvard University. He thereafter continued his studies under other direct disciples of O-sensei, like Koichi

Tohei shihan, Chiba Kazuo shihan and others. An Aikikai 6th dan and 6th dan *kyoshi* in *Muso Shinden Ryu Iaidō*, with over 47 years of experience in martial arts, he opened the Aikidō Center of Los Angeles (ACLA)[1] in 1974 and in 1988 was ordained as a Zen priest.

In 1991, William was selected to serve as one of three *deshi* to Furuya sensei which meant caring for the dōjō and its garden while studying Aikidō, weapons and Muso-shiden-ryu Iaidō daily. In Autumn of 1996, William joined the original Rickson Gracie Academy in Los Angeles, on Pico and Sepulveda, but in February 1997, he left California for Japan to study at the Aikikai Hombu Dōjō. Residing about 300 meters from the dōjō, William lived a simple, even austere life, training three to five times a day, six days a week, for fifteen months, while assisting a former Hombu Dōjō kenshusei teach Aikidō at international schools and private clubs in Tokyo.

William lived and trained in Japan (the first time) for eight years, remains a student of Hombu Dōjō and now again resides in Tokyo. During those initial years, many teachers who were direct students of O-Sensei, such as Ueshiba Kisshomaru Doshu, Arikawa sensei, Ichihashi sensei, Masuda sensei, Tada sensei and others, were still actively teaching at Hombu dōjō, and current senior teachers were quite young and often his training partners.

In 2004, due to a family emergency, William moved to London and began training at London Aikikai, Chiba shihan's old dōjō in the United Kingdom. In 2005, William opened a second home in Beijing and began serving as the senior local instructor to dōjō in Beijing under two Japanese shihan, before starting his own dōjō Beijing Aikikai in 2008 at

---

[1] http://www.aikidocenterla.com

a local MMA academy. William has the unique experience of teaching Aikidō in several MMA Academies in China: Black Tiger, Club Hero and Kunlunjue Fight Club.

To varying levels, William has also studied *Krav Maga* (his law school classmate was Darren Levine, the first American blackbelt), Judō in Britain (from Vasil Panfil) and its derivative art *Brazilian Jujitusu* (having started in 1996 at the Rickson Gracie Academy in Los Angeles and from 2008 at the Roger Gracie Academy in London - who awarded him a blue belt - and also in Beijing at Gracie China where he swapped lessons with the two American black belt instructors, students of Pedro Sauer).

In 2014, William published *Aikidō in Japan and The Way Less Traveled*, a memoir about the Aikikai Hombu Dōjō and his sabbatical training there full time in 1997 and 1998. He is the founder of the YouTube Channel "Aikido Applied" and the new sports/clothing brand "Budōka Gear".

Following the outbreak in Wuhan, William returned to California for nine months but is now living in Japan, training at Hombu Dōjō and studying Japanese *bujutsu*. Although he has lived in five countries on three continents, speaks bits of six languages and studied martial arts for thirty-five years, William swears he is not a spy. Although... is that not exactly what a spy would say? I called William one Tokyo evening this spring 2021. We had a free-flowing, lively and insightful conversation about the state of Aikidō and the world. After all, as his book says, "Go forward. Find your Way!"

*William Gillespie walking the Great China wall*

# Introduction

"Hello everyone. Glad to have you here. Today we have the pleasure of hosting William Gillespie. Welcome William! Nice having you, thank you."

"Well, nice of you to say that and thank you for having me. Now, you think it's good; I don't know about afterward, you may have regrets but thank you for having me."

"No, that's not my kind of thing."

"No buyer's remorse."

"I'm ready to listen. I think there's always something to learn. How is life over there?"

"Good! Today was a good day. It's sunny and nice in Tokyo. I met young *aikidōka* Francesco in the park and did a little bit of weapons and some other practice with him. People are out in Yoyogi Park enjoying it. All kinds of groups. This group doing boxing. That group doing *yoga*. Another doing something else. Then these two strange foreigners with sticks whacking each other. That was us."

"It's nice to see that people there are resilient and they find a way."

"I said to an American friend about the Japanese: when you live in a country that has *kazan* (volcanoes), *ji-shin* (earthquakes) and *typhoons* and *tsunami*, you're not necessarily going to wet the bed over something else that comes along to kill you. They're accustomed to the fact that nature might take them out at any moment. So the response has been different than in my homeland (USA) and or my adopted homeland (UK). Here it's good; it's a good place to be, generally, and right now, particularly."

"I suppose it's a good reminder, no? That we are small and frail."

"Yeah; *memento mori*! Right? Remember you die. There you go, right? The stoics, for sure. You mentioned you read my book and you know I had to deal with the fact my wife was chronically ill for 17 years and literally could fall over at any moment dead, you know, on any given day. Having to deal with that pressure and then also you're already trying to live life, however, it's like being a budōka: you're trying to be engaged in the moment and to be patient with some of your friends for whom this is the first experience with whether to what extent it's really a fact that it could happen to them based on age etc. but you know it's sort of been unsettling, unbalancing for them. They've had to learn how to take *ukemi* and they don't know how to take ukemi. We all know what that first experience was like in the dōjō when we first tried to take ukemi and we didn't know how."

"There's a lot of people out there that are questioning the usefulness of *Budō*; well, here you go this is what it is for."

"Absolutely."

"[Holding up copy of WTG's book Aikidō in Japan and The Way Less Traveled.] Do you know it?"

" [Laughs.] I have to send you a Christmas present now. You're the one guy that bought one!"

"[Laughs.] Oh yeah; that's me. Aikidō in Japan and The Way Less Traveled. I actually truly enjoyed it and I recommend you to all Aikidō lovers."

"Thank you. Thank you. I had to be careful in writing it. There are people in high places and I didn't want them to take it the wrong way. It's really just my experience. I'm not trying to tell people how to do Aikidō: 'This is how you do *ikkyo*, this is how you...' No, not at all. At the end, there's a bit of my experiences teaching in MMA schools in China and also a bit of the colorful nightlife in Japan and different places which people might find interesting but, on the whole, it just tracks the calendar year at Hombu Dōjō, what happens every year in the dōjō, and what happened to me. I also tend to be the butt of most of the jokes in it."

# California

"Let's start from the very beginning. You happened to be born and live in Southern California. This is one of the areas in the world outside of Japan with the strongest Japanese cultural presence. And, this is where you developed as a person, first of all, as an aikidōka and you also had an excellent career there. Could you tell us a little bit about that time of your life in California?"

"Sure. I was born in Southern California, down behind 'The Orange Curtain', as some called notoriously conservative Orange County back then, so I grew up in an outdoors robust kind of culture. It's like whenever I met Australians and South Africans overseas they were swimming or surfing from a young age and were really active. I kind of grew up in that sort of sports culture in California.

"Another distinct thing about the U.S. West Coast was early exposure to Japanese people and their American descendants. In my childhood, Orange County still had orange groves and farms. Two doors down from our house in Anaheim lived a Japanese family who ran a flower farm. Their son was my age and first born in America - '*ni-sei*' (first born out of Japan). So, I had my first 'Japanese' friend at about four or five. Of course, at that age you don't think about these things. I was a little towheaded kid and he's a Japanese kid, but you don't think: 'Oh my friend's Japanese and I'm a blonde Caucasian'. Our hearts are purer then. I do remember thinking: 'Wow! His mom is so calm and pretty. She's so nice.' True to the stereotype of a Japanese American father, his dad loved fishing, baseball and didn't talk much.

"So, you're right, Los Angeles, outside of Japan and São Paulo, has the most people of Japanese descent of any city on the planet and I did have exposure to aspects of East Asian culture at an early age. While I did not realize my interest in martial arts until after I moved north to the San Francisco Bay Area (at seven years old), East Asian culture never felt odd or 'other' to me. Interestingly, our human bias can take many forms and as a result of the move north, I don't really have this So(uthern) Cal(ifornia) No(rthern) Cal(ifornia) hostility that a lot of Californians have because I kind of grew up in both ends of the state.

"It was in No Cal (which has a heavier Chinese influence, in fact) that I initially became keen on martial arts. First, in third grade, I had wanted desperately to join the local *Karate* school but I think my dad thought I would beat up other kids (maybe he was right). Then in 7th and 8th grade I wrestled for my junior high. Back then, California had quite a competitive inter-school sports program. Back in the day, when they weren't handing out trophies to everybody. [Laughs.] There was a really good *Judō* school, Cahill Judō, nearby and I wanted to go. I was interested in going but... and I am guessing... maybe my father, due the potential to bully others and perhaps lingering World War 2 feelings (despite his having Japanese American friends) was still opposed to martial arts? I probably just didn't push hard enough, because he had married someone of German descent and loved all humanity unflinchingly.

Kensho Furuya

William Gillespie training at the Aikidō Center of Los Angeles

*Images from the Aikidō Center of Los Angeles*

"My mom was the first born in America, returned to Germany as a very young child but came back to the States. As a result, I had an immigrant upbringing in many ways. Another language was spoken in our house - German. I knew my grandmother and great-grandmother (Oma and Grossi, both immigrants) and ate German food once a week. There were four generations under one roof every Sunday. From these experiences, new or 'foreign' things were interesting to me, not something to reject out of hand as different.

"Once I could make my own decisions, I tried an Aikidō class in the Mission District in San Francisco. Japanese teacher. I cannot recall his name. It was great but just too far to go because I was living in Burlingame south on the Peninsula. I moved back to So Cal for university and then law school and when I graduated from law school in 1987, I finally went down to Little Tokyo and signed up at an Aikidō dōjō I had learned about from another law student. The dōjō looked like something out of 17th century Japan. The teacher literally shipped in craftsmen from Japan to help him build it in an artist loft that used to be a postal warehouse down by the L.A. River. Daniel Furuya (who would become Kensho Furuya after completing his training for the *Soto Zen* Buddhist priesthood) was the chief instructor. Furuya sensei... he was extraordinary, eccentric, peculiar... you know; different. I'm grateful that he helped set me on this path and it was an interesting and in ways unmatchable martial arts experience in the USA.

"The dōjō was in downtown L.A., in Little Tokyo. At that time, if you wandered about a block to the right or a block to the left, it was like being in *The Walking Dead*, because L.A. 'Skid Row' was very close by and the streets were filled with drug addicts, homeless and the occasional Hispanic gangbanger from East L.A. across the L.A. river. Sensei had two dogs Kuma and Michiko on leashes, in the alley-way out front of the dōjō. Kuma (which means bear in Japanese) had taken out the backside of many trousers. He would chase all the trespassers out of the alley. Once you stepped inside the dōjō, it was another world. Pure zen. Wooden floors, countless antiques, sensei's quarters suspended over the mats, a tea room and more. It was a genuine, colorful, fundamental and forging environment. I just joined and got stuck in training daily. After the first couple of years, he asked if I wanted to become one of three kenshusei – me and two Japanese American students (one his cousin). Just three of us.

"Furuya Sensei was extraordinary. He was 'san-sei', third generation, Japanese American (in the country longer than my family). He began in martial arts as a child in *Kendō* and then at 14 he added Aikidō. He lived in Hombu Dōjō as kenshusei in 1969 for a year. He then went to Harvard and got his master's degree in Japanese studies. While in Boston, he studied with Kanai sensei. When he returned to Los Angeles, among other things, he used to assist Japanese teachers, e.g. Koichi Tohei sensei and others, when they visited California. Later, second *Doshu* asked him to support Chiba sensei as he was setting up in San Diego. He had many Asian American friends in other martial arts like: Fumio Demura (Karate), Danny Inasanto (Bruce Lee's student, *Jeet Kun Do, Escrima*), Hayward Nishioka (Judō), Adam Hsu (*Ba-qua, Tai-qi*) and others. We did about 8 or 9 public demonstrations a summer at various temples and festivals around Los Angeles. I began Muso-shinden ryu Iai-do there as well. Furuya sensei was a real expert on all aspects of the Japanese sword, so much so that he was a qualified appraiser. I was fortunate that I got to train in an extraordinary environment where I was one of a few with direct contact with a high level instructor. I got to train with some very dedicated people. Like I said, I was lucky. It's merely a matter of birth and good fortune, plus some good decisions and overcoming some bad ones. I just happened to be born in

The Traveler - Find Your Way

a good place for learning East Asian culture and Japanese martial arts. I consider myself fortunate."

*Another shot taken at the Aikidō Center of Los Angeles*

*Sadateru Arikawa*

# Good Old Days' Stories

"Could you tell us some story from 'the good old days'? I'm sure that Furuya sensei passed on some." [Laughs.]

"Well; from when he was in Japan? Sure. Arikawa sensei was legendary, even then in 1969. He used to hold himself up by the ceiling straps on the subway and train cars, between stops. He'd grab one with each hand and pull himself up and hold himself suspended between stations as part of his physical training. You know, people like to say 'the whole world's your dōjō' and you can make it such. I do odd things on buses like not hold on and check my balance and all these sorts of things.

"Furuya sensei told me one day that smoking was banned on trains and someone lit up and Arikawa shihan put his hand over the cigarette in the guy's mouth extinguishing it right into the guy's mouth. It was a different place, time and culture. So sensei would tell me these kinds of stories but not too colorful. I know others, like the story of an American who showed up at Hombu Dōjō in 1969 asking to live there and was denied, so he held a grudge for the rest of his life and went on to write prolifically about Aikidō, taking shots at Hombu Dōjō whenever he could. Oh well.

"Japan then, during my teacher's time there, and Japan when I got there, first in '92 and then '94 and then when I moved there at the start of '97, was totally different from Japan today. It is so much more accessible now. 1997 was just the beginning of 'globalization'. For better or worse, the world has shrunk since then; it's become a much smaller place. There are pluses and minuses to this, of course. I touch on that in the book. Especially when considering culture, these days it is important to understand that we have been compressed into a smaller space by jet travel, by the media, by computers, by telecommunications. So, relax and cut each other some slack and get to know each other and over time people reach understandings and accommodations to improve relations between peoples. Things tend to work out.

"Other than Japan, Furuya sensei told stories about the development of Aikidō in Los Angeles, California and the USA. He told me how he quit hanging out with 'celebrities' after a massive parking lot brawl at the Beverly Hills restaurant Trader Vics. He was mentioned in the Hollywood Reporter story for dropping someone who tried to stab him with a broken bottle (probably too many 'Lapu-Lapu Bowls' gulped down by some patrons). Through Furuya sensei, I got to meet other martial artists in *Taekwondo*, Judō, *Naginata*, Kendō, *Wushu* and so on. I met Tamlin Tamita, who was Daniel-san's girlfriend in *Karate Kid 2*. Being in Los Angeles, I didn't really care unless they had real skills. Celebrity alone was boring. While a student at UCLA it was like: 'Oh there's another star. And, another. Who cares'. However, it was interesting to meet other martial artists. I got to experience seminars in our Aikidō dōjō taught by them, like Furuya sensei's good friend Adam Hsu, the well-known Chinese Wushu teacher out of Taiwan.

"I touch on it in the book; I was in Los Angeles when the Gracie Jujitsu craze began. I remember a deshi showing

*Kambe Duruya in his dōjō*

*Jackie Chan and Kensho Furuya*

Furuya sensei the *Gracie in Action* video, as sensei was typing away at his desk. Sensei just stops, folds his arms across his chest, looks up, stares for a minute and says: 'Yeah; that's old Judō' and goes back to typing furiously. He had an encyclopedic mind for martial arts. In 1996, I started BJJ before I moved to Japan. I went to Rickson Gracie's first place in Los Angeles, on Pico and Sepulveda next to the lumberyard. As I like to say, 'got a cup of coffee there'. I went for about three or four months before I moved to Tokyo, but again I was fortunate to be on the west coast, fortunate to be in California. I think that shaped my mind when I meet other people who've really thirsted and struggled to learn but haven't been so blessed to be in the right place with the right people."

# Japan

"At some stage, however, you decided that this Californian experience wasn't really enough."

"True."

"You packed it all and moved to Japan."

"I suppose I had enough of that sunshine and traveling down to Santa Monica beach and going body surfing at the end of the day. I just couldn't stand that anymore."

"I find it hard to believe that. Was there actually a spark? Something that guided it? And, also in general, what motivated you to face such a big change?"

"That's a really good question because when I first got to Japan some Japanese would look at me incredulously and say: 'What? You came from where to do what?'...

"The spark was I went to visit Japan in 1992 and practiced a little bit at Hombu Dōjō. I just felt comfortable there. It's really interesting: there are two places I have visited where I immediately felt very comfortable culturally. One was

Scotland; my father's side of the family is all Scottish. And the other was when I came here. I don't know why, you know, but I did. I loved it. I loved Hombu Dōjō: the pace of practice was really attractive (so fast and relentless back then), all the teachers, so many foreigners from all over the world at that time...

"Next, I visited for a month in '94. What had happened was that I had a fraternity brother from UCLA who was a lawyer also, Doug Raskin. He had moved to Japan (for other reasons) and he was like: 'Come! Move! Quit!'. I had a girlfriend in Los Angeles who was wondering what was next with her. By chance I ran into Doug in a bar in San Francisco January 1994. He listens to my situation and he goes: 'Nah, cut it off, it's not going to work. I just went through that experience before I moved to Japan. Come to Tokyo!' So, I had planned this big trip to visit Doug in May and in March I got this phone call from another friend - it's in the book, in the chapter 'Climb Every Mountain' - and he said: 'Doug's dead'. And when you first hear that, it doesn't make any sense. It's like someone says 'orange juice, cement-mixer, barbecue'. The words don't make any sense in your head. What?

"On the call, I learned Doug had climbed snow-covered Mount Fuji with a bunch of other foreigners in March - not the smartest thing to do outside of climbing season - and he had fallen while taking a photo. Doug was a big guy too, about 6'2 and about 210-215 pounds (so 188 cm and 98 kilos?). As he's taking the picture, a big gust of wind came. It gets incredibly blustery up there. Basically, he's standing on a sheet of ice that starts at the lip of the cinder cone. He had on all the gear, crampons, ice axe, the whole thing. It had seemed calm: he put down the ice axe, stood tall and raised his hands to take the photo and, *poof*, he's gone. He just tumbled [Rotating his finger in the air.] You know, taking ukemi again when you don't know how to take ukemi. Down the mountain! 3,000 feet, so about 1000 meters, dead.

"And then I went to his funeral which was back in Los Angeles. He was Jewish, so we went to the graveside and all of us gathered back from university. And I learned what a great life he had lived since leaving for Japan. He had really touched so many different lives with all the things he'd done. And all these people had come to his funeral service, which was massive, to celebrate his life. Because it's a Jewish service, you go and you actually toss the dirt on your dead friend. You go to the graveside, take your turn with the shovel and dig into the mound of dirt and toss it in on top of the box, at least the way the family marked their faith. I'll tell you that's a reality check.

"Now; I grew up a theologian's kid. I started off as a P.K. - Preacher's Kid - but then my father became a theologian so I became a T.O. - a Theologian's Offspring. [Laughs.] What that does is I had ideas of not only the ever-after but meaning of life and all these kinds of bigger questions in my head since I was a young kid. And so, Doug's funeral took a small spark and fanned the flame to a blazing fire to go to Japan. So, I went on the same trip where I was going to meet him. I traced his life, meeting his friends, etc. I stayed for a month and trained at Hombu as much as possible. Again, I was lucky; I stayed for free with a friend of a friend who ran Merrill Lynch's derivatives desk in Tokyo. I couldn't live like that after I moved here. [Laughs.] His flat was about ten thousand U.S. dollars a month. Massive place.

"During the trip, I decided I loved it and had to live in Tokyo to study Aikidō. I went back to the law firm and two years in a row buried the biggest bonuses they paid. I planned my move and was ready at the end of 1996 but I had a trial at the start of the year, which I felt was my duty to handle. I started off my legal career as a trial lawyer. The trial suddenly settled. I couldn't have been more ecstatic. I was able to ship my things and jump on the plane at the start of February '97. The rest of my things I put in storage.

"The next thing I knew, I was stepping off the Narita Express bus in Tokyo, getting picked up by Tony Hind (former Hombu kenshusei) and wondering if I'd done the right thing! [Laughs.] Half the people I knew thought I was a genius, the other half thought I was crazy and probably both were half right. I never looked back."

"You left a job that was… Can you remind me how much you were making at your firm?"

"I was making, in current dollars, about 300 000 U.S. dollars a year and I wasn't even a partner yet. I was on the right track and all that, but I 'put my money where my mouth is'. Whether my mouth was in the right place, I don't know but I put my money where my mouth is and gave it up."

"It's not all about money, I suppose…"

"Well better to try than, you know, reach 70 or, if I make it that far, 80 or 90 and go with regret, 'My God I could have been a contender!'. It's better to just go do what you want to do and then sort it out as things go along. So, I did it."

Tony Hind

# The Training Culture at the Aikikai Hombu Dōjō

"Could you describe for us the training culture that you found at Hombu Dōjō? At the beginning did you experience any difficulties to integrate? Based on your actual experience, what does it really take to become a good and effective deshi at the Aikikai Hombu Dōjō? We know it's unlike any other dōjō in the world."

"Look, I'm not a deshi or a kenshusei but when I went to Japan I did try to copy that kind of lifestyle. I had a lot of money in the bank. I didn't have to work. I was able to train two to five times a day and the only reason for two would be that I was helping Tony Hind teach someplace else.

"Tony 'The Truth' Hind... He's an experience. To say about him 'he's a strong guy', the reply would be 'yeah and the Grand Canyon is a big hole in the ground'. It doesn't quite describe the experience. He's a person who boxed before he did Aikidō and he played first division rugby in Canada and was a winger, which means he's 'twitchy': you know, fast twitch muscle. About 184 centimeters and about 99 kilos, so.... people found him difficult to train with on a regular basis. [Laughs.] Imagine that. Thanks to my Scottish side, I just got stuck in and trained with him and I thought: 'This guy beating the stuffing out of me can be really good for me'. That and 'F*** me that hurt,' So I was helping him around Tokyo a couple days a week and then training the rest of the time. On Sundays I rested.

"I had gone to Tokyo and Hombu twice before in 1992 and 1994, so I knew what to expect, to a certain degree. My first teacher was very fundamental. His fundamentals were along the lines of Kisshomaru Doshu. Furuya sensei had his 'own Aikidō' as well, which he would express in demonstrations. So, I wasn't entirely unaware of what to expect.

"I've seen many people come into Hombu for the first time. We used to call them 'new meat'. They would come in, not being used to the hard mats, not being used to the fast practice and we'd pounce on some of them. If they were nice, we wouldn't do that, but if they weren't, then 'clobberin time'. Although I knew what to expect to some degree, it was tough to train that often. However, it was a different time than now. The world's changed a lot. Japan's changed a lot and Aikidō's changed a lot. One of the most difficult challenges for Aikidō now is the talent drain. When I arrived in 1997 (until I left in 2004), it hadn't happened yet. There were still a lot of really strong, physically strong, people on the mats at Hombu Dōjō. The problem now is that you can only make the best pot you can out of whatever clay you've got. Or the best sword you can, out of the best iron you've got and all other ingredients and processes that go with it. Any one input slips and so does the quality of the output. That's a genuine challenge now.

"Then, I found Hombu Dōjō challenging in this respect. The students were very robust, like what you find these days in an MMA school or BJJ school or Judō. Also, now still, there are so many students, hundreds, and you do not know them all and that affects training. In my old dōjō, for example, because you're kenshusei and because you've been there a while and it's a smaller group, you tend to make accommodations for each other in training. This can happen. You know each other. You know each others technique. You know how to respond. You know not to push too far. There can be too much cooperation.

"However, there's a certain amount of anonymity at a place like Hombu Dōjō, which can be very big and very cold, which frankly I think is very good for a lot of the people that come from their home dōjō and feel very proud of themselves that they are something special at home. Then they come there and they find out they're just not that special. They're just another foreigner coming to learn."

"A wake up call."

"Yeah; it's a good experience for anybody and I think I found those things a bit challenging and then of course I got there and in my first practice I got into a fight with a deshi (now a friend of mine). [Laughing.] He's now a shihan. We got into a full-on fight in the back. We ended up wrestling on the ground with people separating us. [Laughing.] It was a different age. Your experience there may still depend on where you sit at the start of class. I mention this in the book. The mat's big, right? What is it? Eighty *tatami*? Something like that? More? I can't remember. In this corner, people were killing each other. In one corner, you had some more experienced teachers. For example, in Kisshomaru Doshu's Friday night class you had people like Kato sensei coming in and others coming in to pay their respects and support the dōjō. That's in the back corner on the left-hand side. On the left-hand side and toward the front? That's a different kind of animal you were coming in touch with and all of us 'crazy monkeys' in the back in the right corner, you know, *shikaku*, the 'death corner', we were all by the men's changing room. It used to be like that but it's not like that anymore. So, you could sit down and bow in and have a really rough hour of 'travel', if you weren't careful." [Laughing.]

"Depending on who you picked."

"Correctamundo."

"The amazing thing is the mixture. If you actually want to train pensioner-style you can."

"Yep. Yes; absolutely. Absolutely. It's not like people didn't know what they're getting into. You knew it, once you were there for a while. If you're going at it with one of your rougher or stronger friends then that's the way it was going to be, 'no quarter given no quarter asked for'. Of course, you'd be appalled if you actually hurt the person. However, you trained as if you're really going to get them. And, they're really trying to get you. That's the way we trained, at least the Aikidō as an applied martial art crowd.

"It was funny; I was having dinner after BJJ and Aikidō class in Beijing (I did the BJJ class and then taught the Aikidō class at the MMA academy) with a friend, a big Canadian guy, Ken, that used to visit Beijing for business and do the BJJ classes. Turns out, he used to live in Japan and trained at Hombu Dōjō and we had mutual friends. So, after class, we go out with a South African friend of mine, BJJ brown belt, and Ken is describing *asa-keiko*, the 06:30 morning class, to the BJJ guy. He's like, 'you grab your friend as hard as you can and he throws you as hard as he can, four times in a row, and then your friend grabs you and you throw him as hard as you can, four times in a row'. The BJJ guy's eyes are getting bigger and bigger, you know. He's just laying on the ground and rolling and having fun, a laugh with his mates. Of course, it's hard too but it's not the same experience as getting slammed on the mat at 06:30 in the morning, on a cold winter day in Tokyo. On mats that are like concrete." [Laughing.]

"That's actually one of the things that not many mention but it's possibly one of the biggest problems you have when you come from outside and you start training at the Hombu. The mats are so hard that it's like falling on a concrete slab."

"Yeah, on concrete and then they're like sandpaper. So don't let someone rub your face on them. Often, there was blood on them after class."

*William Training at the Aikikai Hombu Dojo in his early days*

*Kensho Furuya*

# Furuya Sensei's Helping Hand

"Going back to the Californian experience, when you moved to Japan, was there anything that coming from California and Aikidō with Furuya sensei that actually helped you? Because I heard of maybe some disadvantages for foreigners? Was there something that actually made it easier for you given your past experience?"

"Well, I think Furuya sensei was a psychological stickler. He was a stickler for etiquette and all these kinds of things and that was very helpful. He was an expert at putting psychological pressure on you. Some people these days would say: 'Oh you're abusing me'. No, no, no. It's part of being forged, learning to perceive and intuit when things were ambiguous or otherwise unclear yet you were required to act: quickly, decisively and properly. There are a lot of teachers that are good at popping you [shows his fist], if you do the wrong thing and that happened to me too, but he was very bright, right? Maybe too smart. He was expert at applying *atsu*, pressure, on you (the kenshusei mostly) like this and that, plus the physical training, develops fortitude.

"For example, in my work, I noticed when I went to court, especially federal court... You know what's the difference between God and a federal district court judge, who is appointed for life? God doesn't think he is a federal district court judge. In other words, a federal district judge thinks he's God. So I noticed that when I started to go to court that Aikidō had changed me. I was no longer fearful or nervous. I became like, 'Well, whatever's going to happen. If I take it in the neck and the judge wants my wallet or puts me in jail, there I go'. So, I think when I got to Japan, I wasn't frightened by psychological discomfort, including the difference or the otherness of it. I think it can be, you know, unsettling for people. Especially Tokyo can be unsettling because it has a veneer of seeming western-ness in some respects, so it looks like it ought to be. You think it ought to be a certain way but it's not working that way at all.

"I can remember on my first trip in 1992, where suddenly - I forget the teacher's name - he just comes up to me after the morning class, while waiting for 08:00 class, and yells at me - he'd seen me before - that this other foreigner is leaning against the center post just relaxing between classes. My Japanese wasn't that good yet and I'm like okay I think I figured it out. 'Yo dude, stop leaning on the post'. I think that dealing with those kinds of ambiguities, pushing yourself out into the deep water, challenging yourself with uncertain circumstances is how you grow, because martial arts are not just a physical component, especially if you're talking about confrontations that aren't necessarily in the context of match fighting or ring fighting. It's much more unclear and uncertain. You're walking down the street someplace or such, and I think that Furuya Sensei's dōjō prepared me for those sorts of experiences.

"I also think that I had a very orthodox, very fundamental Aikidō, which was an asset when I arrived. It is helpful to have a solid base before arriving. However, I think, at that point in my development, I gained more by being in Japan - for a lot of

*Kensho Furuya - uke William Gillespie*

*Hiroshi Tada*

reasons. At Hombu, I got a new perspective, and saw different aspects of Aikidō. The great thing about Hombu, that used to be, is that: the teacher is the swordsmith, the *tatara* (the furnace) is the dōjō's method and style of practice, the ore and other things are the students and Hombu had the first two plus a critical mass of students. Every Aikidō geek in the world, practically, was there or visited. And, they had all these different masters that would help to shape you in different ways. You'd see some new aspect in a teacher's technique that you hadn't seen before. When I arrived, of course, Nidai Doshu was still teaching and Arikawa sensei was teaching and so was Tada sensei and Ichihashi sensei (each a student of O-sensei), so you received different deep perspectives on Aikidō.

"And then, there was the emphasis on *suwari-waza* and constantly sitting just in life and being trained by the cultural aspects of life in Japan. My apartment was a six tatami mat room. I sat on the ground all the time. I walked everywhere. I didn't have the brains to buy a bike the first year, so I was walking to the dōjō at 05:30 daily. Again I have to use this metaphor of forging yourself: those kinds of things were great experiences. Life was harder. In Los Angeles, I had my car. Just drive to the dōjō to put in two hours of practice. Drive home. Sit in chairs. This experience in Japan was something more encompassing because of the culture. I would say that I had been grounded in very orthodox fundamentals to begin with and that was very helpful. It gave me a good base upon which to build much more."

*Kisshomaru Ueshiba*

# Asa-keiko, the Morning Class

"You already mentioned asa-keiko, the morning class, and in your book you explain the importance of it at the Hombu Dojo. It's been a favorite for thousands of Aikidō students from all over the world. Could you elaborate a little about it and explain for the reader why asa-keiko is so important?"

"Sure. At that time it was led by Nidai Doshu, when he was getting older, so people wanted to go and show their respects but I think that it's the blueprint. It shows the blueprint for what Aikidō is. And you're going to get a broad exposure, a good sampling of the basic curriculum, if you attend five days a week. That's number one, okay? It's a great way to polish your fundamentals. It's also a great way to start the day. It takes the personal discipline of getting up every day and going and doing something that's inconvenient. I think, in learning anything in life, if you practice when it's inconvenient, you'll end up getting as good as you can get at it. So, I would say number one, it's kind of the blueprint for Aikikai Aikidō. That doesn't mean it's going to cover all the curriculum but it's going to give you a solid base and exposure to a key portion of it. I'd also say that this is how the deshi are trained: they go every morning.

"And then, if you have the time, what I would do is I'd sneak down to the second floor at 07:30 and I'd do the remainder of the beginner's class because then I could watch Miyamoto sensei move slowly with beginners. And I could train with beginners and feel how real people move - not like Aikidō people. Then I'd run back up the stairs for the 08:00 class where another senior teacher came in to teach.

"Another consideration, in terms of how you're perceived by others, is that by doing the morning class you're perceived as being '*majime*', as being serious. You're a serious student, because you're putting yourself through this inconvenient, difficult task of getting up every day. Remember, when you get here, in most cases, they don't know you. Your reputation is built on your observable behavior, principally your attendance and actions on the mats. Believe me: any measure of tolerance they have for me has been because I just put in the bloody hard work. Later, I had a really lovely wife, who they all liked, and I often said that I married her so people would like me. It's kind of like tying a steak around your neck and being around dogs or something."

"I must be good: look!" [Laughs.]

"Yeah; I know. [Laughs.] 'Well, he must not be all bad, after all.' Again, I would say that those are other reasons to do it. I think number one is you're showing your sincerity and that's a huge thing in Japan. The second thing is you're a reliable person; you're a serious person. Even though you might like to joke and have fun, you're also a serious person. It also shows a commitment to practice and you're getting this perspective or a sampling of the techniques from someone who's showing them to you in a very kind of vanilla way. They're not injecting a lot of their personality into it. There's a continuity between each generation of Doshu, so I think that's why I would attend if you have the time to do it.

"Would you say that asa-keiko, the morning classes are like *iemoto*[2] in action? Like the continuity of the tradition in action from iemoto?"

"Yeah; iemoto. I think so too. There's that and there's this aspect of paying respect to someone. Even if you just did it for a year and then you decided, well asa-keiko doesn't work for me with my job now, you've already kind of set the tone of who you are. I think that's another way to describe it.

"It doesn't mean that's what you have to do though. I mean, my book says: 'Find your Way', right? I don't mean to be corny about that: it's just that that's where I think you have the self-expression that everybody's so desperate to do. Within the context of how you develop yourself, that's where you find your own self-expression. Deciding to add things and change techniques? I see people that have been doing Aikidō – often superficially – for 15 years telling me how they're going to modernize it? [Puts finger to his head like a gun and pulls the trigger.] You know? I just want somebody to [slashes at head like a *katana* decapitating him]. It just makes your head explode. I'm like: 'Really? That's all you're doing? Why not cure cancer? Why aim for that?' You know?"

[Both laughing]

"Yeah. [Laughing] 'Making it better'. Yes."

"Well, you know; people! Anyway, that's why I would do the morning class."

---

[2] Iemoto, 家, meaning literally "family foundation", is a term that can be used for the leader of a Japanese cultural tradition, Grand Master in English, and a system for preserving that tradition through leaders of successive generations of a family.

William Gillespie

# Balancing Life in Tokyo

"Again, let's go back to the beginning of your experience – even though your experience has been a little different from the normal one. Most people that moved to Japan report having a lot of problems because they want to train, first of all, but then they discover they have to juggle..."

"Right, correct."

"The reality of life means that even though training may be your number one, you also need to support yourself, therefore work. And another very important thing: you cannot live in foreign country without mastering the language, so learning Japanese. How does it relate to your experience? How did you manage? And any advice for people that want to follow the same path?"

"Sure. Some of it I managed well; some of it I didn't. I mean looking back now. And then, I made some of the same mistakes when I ended up in China. I would say that, number one, I was lucky. I had socked away a bunch of money so I didn't have to worry about work. Maybe I spent more money than wiser people would want to spend, but I had the freedom to train for 15 months."

"Money is never enough, right?"

"Yeah; that's true. So, I was lucky that first year. I wasn't married yet. It took me forever to settle down. Once the Peter Pan suit got a bit tight I figured I'd better get married and grow up. [Both laugh.] Anyway, I was really lucky that I wasn't distracted by other things. I didn't have a job. I didn't have a wife. I didn't have a girlfriend. I had a girlfriend but she was living in Korea and that came later. I could really just focus on training for the first 15 months but then you're right. Reality settled in, so I went back to working as a lawyer but I had to strike the right balance.

"The first job didn't really work out so well and then I was lucky again. I landed a job where they're like: 'Well we can't afford to pay you, you've got too much experience, blah, blah'. My answer was: 'Don't worry about it. Just so I don't have to do any *sa-bi-su zangyo* (service overtime). I just have to work from 09:30 to 05:00 and I'm out of here, right?'. Also, living in Los Angeles, I had learned that it's important where you live to minimize your commute time. Make that as smooth and swift as possible. So, from the office, I had just two stops on the subway, one easy line change, and two stops to the dōjō. Leave a bike at the station and I could still make Miyamoto shihan's class on Fridays and do Doshu's at 7 pm. During the rest of the week, I was able to do asa-keiko or somebody else's evening class, plus Saturdays, and thereby perpetuate what I had been doing.

"I would say that in the area of learning the language, I studied Japanese before I left Los Angeles but, of course, that was pretty much useless once I got to Japan because I wasn't using it enough. And then I made a mistake in Tokyo. I decided to join a school but made a mistake about what school I joined. Now people are more fortunate that the internet is so full of different ways to study online that weren't quite available yet.

"I arrived in sort of the infancy of the internet. The best thing was a video of a monkey scratching its butt and sniffing it and falling out of a tree. That still might be the best thing on the internet. [Laughing] So it's a trade-off. I had lots of advantages but there were disadvantages too and I think that getting into the right school is key. It is worthwhile to go to Japanese school to help give you a little bit more structure to your day. You can also get a visa that way.

"It's never been easier to go to Japan. If you're in your 20s, my God, you're going to be 30 one day. Why not be 30 and have lived in Japan? If you're 30 why not turn 40 having lived in Japan? Same thing as you go up the ladder. It's just a matter of being able to arrange it and it's never been easier to arrange. I would say though that I made mistakes as you read in the book when I talked about Japanese language. You know the story about the NHK guy (Japanese National TV). That's a true story, about my friend who opened the door naked."

"Give it to us!" [Laughing]

"A buddy of mine is a Canadian; we call him the MacGyver of Tokyo because if you gave him some duct tape, some paper clips and a stapler, he could build an aircraft carrier. This guy is just amazing, right? Some of the readers probably know who he is. The government used to check up on you whether or not you had a television, it's like the TV license in the UK, okay? And, you had to pay this TV fee and, if you get here as a foreigner and you're not bilingual, you don't understand a bloody thing on Japanese TV. Half the foreigners would stuff their television into the closet and say: 'Look; I got no TV' to avoid the fee.

"So, going back to my buddy, his NHK guy kept coming back. He wouldn't take 'No TV' for an answer. So, what does my friend do? He's a rather plump big guy. When the NHK guy came and knocked on the door, my friend answered the door stark naked. Just whipped open the door and said: '*Irashai*!' 'Come on in!', right? That NHK guy looked like a blue-uniformed streak sprinting down the street. Never came back again.

"So to my NHK guy, I opened the door and acted like I was searching for the right words and blurted out: '*Nihongo wo tabemasen*', which means 'I don't eat Japanese language', and grinned proudly. He just went like: 'Oh forget it. It's not worth my time coming back here again' [Both Laughing]. I don't know if they come around anymore. I'm not sure how it would work now. They're probably much wiser about it and speak English to you and say: 'Look; pay the fee, bub'. "

"Things have changed. I remember, maybe 20 years ago, when I first came to Ireland, once I was driving and I forgot my driver's license at home but I had my Italian ID on me. Completely different from any international driver's license. I managed to convince the policeman that the ID was the Italian driver's license: 'OK! Off you go!'." [Laughing]

"Living abroad one has to improvise from time to time."

不和
同而

*William Gillespie*

*Morihei Ueshiba*

# Living With O-sensei's Legacy in Japan

"Change of subject now: let's talk a bit about the founder Morihei Ueshiba, a very complex character, nowadays experienced in the West by the Aikidō community with a mixture of respect and reverence that sometimes, or often, I have to say, borders on... it's a big word but idolatry. It would be interesting to know how this relates to the situation in Japan. How does the Japanese contemporary Aikidō community relate to the figure and the memory of the founder?"

"That's a really interesting question and, yeah, I think the idea of idolatry can be an issue. You know, everybody loves superheroes. There's a reason behind some of the most popular films these days but then you have the cultural aspects. I think that westerners can still be a bit naive about the Far East. It seems unclear and mystical to us and perhaps we're easily enamored with these kinds of things. It's not a criticism. It's just the way it is.

"I mean, they sometimes may feel the same toward us. There are things that are very attractive about our Western culture and background and history and, you know, it's just a part of human curiosity. And, we all love to dream and kind of fantasize about things and love adventures and stories but I think, in the case of Japanese, a cultural difference would be that they don't feel the need to express everything, you know, verbally. Usually, there's what they think personally and then there's what they're actually going to say publicly or in a group, unless you get them really pissed (drunk) and then they might tell you what they really think. And then the next day everybody forgets it."

"*In Vino Veritas!*"

"Right; truth in wine. What can I teach to a Roman! [Laughs] So it's an interesting idea I do still come across here. I think you don't come across as much nihilism, as you do typically in the west these days. You don't come across that and I don't think they're afflicted with our narcissism either, which has been growing. I mentioned that in the book right? You know, the psychological test for narcissism? The drastic uptick in Western society?

"So, O-sensei, is a person who does all these amazing things in his life and then there's a guy online, in his mom's basement, in his underwear, complaining about him? Who are you? So, I think that's one difference. They tend to suffer less from delusions of grandeur. There may be thoughts that they have on their own vs. what they will say publicly. I mean, O-sensei is still venerated; still respected. And, I think that some of the concepts that we westerners like to have determined very definitively - I mean, you're really seeing this in the West now, where you have these ridiculous dichotomies, these ridiculous sorts of bipolar ideas. It's all this way or it's all that way. Culturally here, people are, I think, more adept at dealing with ambiguities and not expressing every thought they have.

"It's not the kind of thing that all of us talk about all the time. To the extent that someone would have reservations or criticisms, here they'll often keep it to themselves because they think it would be disrespectful to other people. It's the issue of 'face', right? There's big differences in face between China, Japan and Korea too, by the way. I've learned firsthand how that cultural idea plays out within the actual society. In the West, you have a lot of people just expressing their opinion, but you also have a lot of iconoclasts who want to tear everything down. I mentioned nihilism and narcissism that makes people think that what they have to say matters.

"O-sensei lived in a time you can't even recreate today. First of all, it's difficult to even comprehend what he lived through. Most people's lives are so easy and so convenient now. The notion of doing the things he did is just beyond what your typical westerner can comprehend, especially some younger 'oppressed' person who's been immersed in post-modernist notions pushed by the Frankfurt School. And then again, how does any of this relate back to your practice? For me, as an American - I also have British citizenship and my own cultural traditions as well - I'm not inclined to place people on a pedestal. I come out of the Judeo-Christian tradition of the West and we're taught not to venerate people to the point of idolatry. That's the right word; I think that's definitely the right word. And you see this in other martial arts, I don't know, you can pick, even when they're not in Japan. You can see this kind of deification of people and I think you don't need to go that far but you can still say: 'Hey, look: this person was an amazing human being, you know, in terms of his quest trying to understand existence and trying to understand conflict in human life - of which he saw his fair share - and trying to understand how he could develop himself'.

"I think if all of us would spend more time trying to take the log out of our own eye to help take the speck out of your brothers or sisters, we'll be a lot better off. There's too much finger wagging and fault finding at everybody around us and not enough of turning it back on ourselves and trying to improve what I do and how I interact in the world and how that enhances the lives of those with whom I interact.

"Bringing it back to your question, it's not the kind of thing that they really will talk about, although I've heard people say: 'Look people, he's not Emperor Palpatine of Star Wars shooting rays out of his fingers and knocking people down'. You know, O-sensei was a man, like anyone else. He was an incredibly strong man and an incredibly well-trained person and, in many different respects, not just a martial artist. It should be an inspiration for what a human being can become through training, how you can take human beings and train them rather than just make an app or a machine that can do the job that a human being can do. I almost sound like Frank Herbert in *Dune*, but that's kind of my take on it. I don't have that much to say specifically on the question. I've had people express to me and say: 'Oh you know he's not tossing people around the room when he's 83 years old' and I've had other people tell me: 'I saw some amazing things by an older gentleman that I just couldn't believe and couldn't get my head around'. So, I answered your question without answering your question or offending anyone; for once."

"The Japanese way…"

"Yeah; it's a first for everything; let me tell you." [Laughing.]

*Morihei Ueshiba*

*Kisshomaru Ueshiba*

# The True Greatness of Kisshomaru Ueshiba

"Let's stay with the Ueshibas now. Let's talk about Nidai-Doshu. There's no doubt, in my mind anyway, that he, his foresight, his understanding that Aikidō needed to be modernized - let's use the bad word 'changed' - in order to succeed as an art that could be suitable for the late 20th century society, that these actions were decisive for the success of Aikidō. Basically, it's thanks to him that you and I are talking here today."

"100% correct. Yeah; absolutely."

"No Nidai Doshu? Then Aikido disappears in some dōjō, some place, up a mountain or so. Kisshomaru Ueshiba could have stayed an employee in his company and all of this would not have taken place. Thanks to his work, there's been millions of people training in Aikidō worldwide. This is one side of the argument. The other side of the argument is that whenever we talk about Aikidō and especially about its great teachers, everyone (back to what we were just saying) is ready to state how great Morihei Ueshiba was, while Kisshomaru sensei is considered like an obscure figure sometimes barely mentioned, especially when you compare him to his father. Could a case be made that maybe he was the real O-sensei?"

"Well, gosh. Again, I think a lot of people have a lot of opinions that are a lot of nonsense. What's the best thing about the internet? Everybody has an opinion. What's the worst thing about the internet? Everybody has an opinion. That's what I wanted to say about idolatry and O-sensei, right, or deification and O-sensei. So what effect does that have on me now? Everyone wants to complain. Anyone can destroy anything. Anyone can tear anything down. I think one of the worst problems we have in the United States is that intellectually we've been fed all this critical theory and all you do is criticize and destroy and take things down and that's why you see destruction of everything; it reminds me of... I won't say. 'Destroy the four olds'. You can Google that yourself. Anyway, I think that Kisshomaru sensei, in his own right, was a great teacher. He was a great man, that's for sure. I mean, I met him numerous times and he was one of the most dignified human beings I've ever been around. And he also developed so many of the teachers that took Aikidō global. He knew how to make a student. He knew how to make a teacher.

"Now, there's no question that O-sensei is this complex, amazing avatar. It's almost hard to describe him. I mean how can any of us even relate to it? Because we haven't done all the things he's done. It is very difficult to articulate and encapsulate him but he's a sort of burst of creativity, or genius and then you have someone else (Kisshomaru sensei) who comes along to nurture it, grow it, sustain it and to focus it in a way. You know, there were monumental historical things going on at the time. You have World War 2 and all related (and it could have ended Aikidō).

"Then, you're right; you have to think about change... but I would use the word 'accessibility' rather than modernization because the world wasn't all that modern at that point. Yeah, it had new ways to blow each other up; sure, but I would say 'make it accessible' and make it accessible to non-Japanese, non-East Asians. I tend to use the word East Asian because Asia's a big place: Russians, Eurasians and Indians are Asians and Pakistanis are Asians and from all over the place right? So I think that you're correct in the idea that he's the reason that we're doing this and I think it's okay that you don't have to be another creative teacher. We've had the creative genius. We've had the spark of ingenuity, okay. It's like O-sensei is the person who finds and plants the seed and Nidai Doshu comes along and nurtures it. I walked through Shinjuku Park recently and there's this view of a pond and the sakura and the other blossoms and foliage. It is wonderful but then they built a pavilion which, if you sit in, gives you the proper view from which to see best and benefit. Likewise, in a way, Kisshomaru Doshu brought Aikidō into focus for people. It doesn't matter 'Is he the strongest?'. I used to hear this kind of thing in a BJJ academy I trained in - I won't say which one. A younger student was complaining he thought he could beat one of the black belts; so how does he have a black belt? And I'm like, no, it doesn't work like that. It doesn't really work like that and my feeling is that you've hit the nail exactly on the head. Kisshomaru Doshu has really taken this new creation and nurtured it and grown it into something that's accessible for more people to do. His objective was to maximize participation? Maximize benefit to society? Then what he did with the original creation is in its own way commendable. It doesn't have to be identical to his father. You don't have to compare him to his father. People want to criticize Nidai Doshu. Why? You wouldn't be doing Aikidō, if it wasn't for him."

"Because you mentioned earlier the fact that most people love superheroes and there's no doubt in my mind that Morihei was our superhero. His son doesn't qualify at all, because he has been doing a different kind of work that is possibly even more important than what the superhero does, because without it we wouldn't have anything. Nonetheless, this doesn't appeal to the imagination of people. Maybe we should start calling Kisshomaru Doshu O-sensei the Second..."

"I don't know, but what does it matter? How does it affect your practice? I mean that's the other thing. It's like, you know, one more thing to argue about. Let me tell you. When you get on your deathbed - I'm not there yet but I've been around people that have been - you're not going to wish: 'If only I had one last discussion about whether or not O-sensei could do this or that'. I used to joke about it with a friend. I said: 'You know how many aikidōka does it take to change a light bulb? Just one and all the rest to tell you how O-sensei did it. And then dear Stan Pranin to tell you only Saito sensei knew how. [Laughing]

"At the end of the day, this doesn't affect you. It's just this silly nonsense of whether Spiderman can beat Underdog in a fight. Get it out of your head, because I got news for you: [whispering] they're both fictional. Spoiler alert! They're fake." [Laughter]

*Kisshomaru Ueshiba*

AIKIKAI

合気道

IWATA CO.
TRADE MARK
TOKYO
MADE IN JAPAN

# The Yin/Yang of the Grading System in Aikidō

"Another interesting topic: everyone loves to get promoted. That's why it is endemic, yes? Are Aikidō gradings and ranks a necessary evil?"

"That's another interesting question. Someone asked me one year why I got promoted to sixth dan and I said: 'Because I have my mother's Germanic gift with people'. [Laughter.] So, I'm the wrong person to ask about how to get promoted. Believe me. I've had to clear the bar by extra feet and wrest the certificate out of their hands before they got close enough to the shredder due to second thoughts. [Laughter]

"Again, you've got people who just want to tear everything down. I get it. Look; I'm where I am and I promised one of my students I wouldn't say anything controversial [Laughs] so I won't but in other countries in the world? Definitely not in East Asia! There are countries where they have dōjō that they call a 'McDojo' or they call them 'HP Dojo' because they have a Hewlett Packard printer that just spews out the certificates. (It's probably a global phenomenon.) I don't think the Aikikai's gotten that bad yet but I do remember Furuya sensei told me that at Hombu Dojo... and there's a difference between if you're a Hombu Dojo student when you get promoted and if you're someplace else in Aikikai... that's for sure. Not zero to four, okay? And, he told me it used to be really hard to get fourth dan at Hombu; really hard, back in the day. And, I was in Hombu Dojo when somebody failed *yondan* three times. Three times! And the guy, from Iran, went: 'Oh you're racists!' and I said to him: 'No, hey, come here man. I got some news for you. It's not that good: it's not. I got news for you mate, it's not them; it's you. But here's the good part. If you practice harder, you can fix it'.

"I think also in the West we're struggling a lot with dominance hierarchies. 'Tear them all down! They're all bad!'. They're not necessarily. I think that promotions can provide a structure and structure can provide safety and a sense of responsibility and nurturing those who are behind you. It depends. One of the worst problems is someone that gets a promotion because they've taken care of the bookkeeping and gotten, you know, the student applications done and suddenly they get their fifth dan... And now they think they're Iron Man. So that is a problem but then what do we do about it? I still think that maybe it's become a bit too easy and after a while it has no meaning. I've seen people in countries where they're getting promoted to fifth dan in just 18 years of marginal training and they've never had a teacher before. I mean, they had a teacher long distance, occasionally. They visited once a year in Japan for a week and that teacher came to their home country for a weekend a year. There are exceptions to the rules. There are people that catch on like that but... On the other hand, you're trying to build a structure and you're trying to build a community in a country and you're trying to do all these things to develop the art.

"I think, on a personal level, that it's good having milestones. I noticed doing BJJ that they give you the stripe on the belt. Everybody's so happy about that: 'Oh; I got a cookie.' It's human nature and so I think on the one hand you should still have them but on the other hand we should maybe make it tougher. However, I don't know if you can go back now that the genie is out of the bottle. Maybe the gradings have become a bit too easy? Past a certain level, like after fourth dan? Maybe before that? This is another problem we're having - equality of opportunity versus equality of outcome. Equality of outcome is not guaranteed in life and it's a very boring life if you decide to orient your society that way. I can go to Michael Jordan's basketball camp, in my case it was John Wooden's, from now till the cows come home, even if I was 18 years old, and it's not going to make me Michael Jordan. And that's not a bad thing. Speaking of John Wooden[3], for anybody who's teaching, go study him: he was almost teaching basketball like it was an eastern martial art. His definition of success is incredible to understand in your own life. Basically, it's peace of mind in knowing that you've done the best, your utmost, under the circumstances given your abilities. In life, that's all you can do.

"So rounding back, I think we've seen this issue of the gradings becoming easier in all martial arts as they were commercialized. We saw this with Taekwondo and more recently even in BJJ. It used to be super hard to get a blue belt and it became easier and easier and easier. Aikidō's been no different in that regard. I think particularly the problem or the challenge with Aikidō is how do you maintain standards when there's no competition? But then again we get back to this survival of the fittest attitude and this utilitarian attitude that if I can't win the match that means I'm not the best or the best teacher. Well, that's not necessarily true. Some of the people that are the best teachers aren't really that gifted and oftentimes it's because they weren't so gifted that they had to dig in deeper and study harder and then convey that to another person in a way that can develop them. I think there's some valid criticism that perhaps we should make it a bit more

[3] www.coachwooden.com

challenging for people. If people are worried about numbers declining, I don't think you're going to help the art by just making it easier and easier and easier and easier."

"No, because you're actually developing an inverted pyramid. You know? In my younger days, when I started Aikidō, at the beginning of the 70s, it used to be that in Italy there were two resident Japanese shihans; initially they had a fifth dan and they got promoted to sixth dan, right? Plenty, tons of people were training under them. Tons, okay? I remember when my dad[4] got third dan in 1979 it was like 'wow'. Now everyone is 'meh'. I don't even know how many seventh dans we got in Italy now, but in the meantime the base actually shrunk a lot. There's many high ranked practitioners, therefore you would expect that the base also expanded as a consequence. That didn't happen. That's a big problem."

"I know: I've seen it. I've been in a country where they're trying to develop an Aikidō community and develop Aikidō enthusiasts. It was so difficult to learn. In Beijing, it started in 2002. A local guy just started this big group but who taught him? Nobody; he was trying to make money. And then another guy, a Russian friend of mine, quite a good boxer, now out of China, who later joined my dōjō, he knew another kind of offshoot of Aikidō and he was starting to teach too. Aikikai arrived as well and within three years people got black belts. I don't think that helped anybody. I struggle with this with my own students now. I tell them: 'No. You're not getting promoted that fast; sorry'. If you want that, go to one of the other places. If they go, that means they don't belong in my group. Mind is wrong. If I send one of my kenshusei to a seminar there, the 'quick dans' won't practice with them. I think there are a few fourth dans now and maybe even two

---

[4] Danilo Chierchini, pioneer of Aikido in Italy, helped Hiroshi Tada to get established in Italy. He reached the rank of 5th and was a founding member, vice president and president of the Italian Aikikai.

fifth dans? Good Lord; it blows your mind. They won't go near my students because they know it's fake. How is that good for them? Martial arts should dispel our delusions, not create or foster them.

"Culture works into it too and all this kind of thing; it has nothing to do with my liking or disliking a place. I teach a certain way in China out of respect. I'm not babying them. I tell them this all the time. 'I'm doing it this way because Chinese people can do anything like anybody else, maybe better. They don't have to be babied. You don't need me to go: 'There, there, child. Here's another promotion'. What patronizing nonsense – the subtle discrimination of low expectations. I don't want it to all be a big joke there. I want people to be capable and skilled. Why not? So when they hear that, a lot of them will go: 'Oh, I like that', 'That makes sense'. And, those are the ones I want to stay. They understand my strictness comes from affection and respect.

"I've been a little more flexible about dōjō outside of Beijing that are in my group, but all in due time. It's a process, but in my own dōjō I've been strict and I think they've gotten better and stronger and you know when one of them comes here to Hombu Dojo and a shihan says: 'He's not bad', that is high praise from a Japanese. If I can create two or three people like that and then disappear into the mists of time, great. This will be my little gift back to China which has provided us with a lot of really great times and experiences.

"I think you're onto something and we have to come up with a solution for this: you can't just keep making it easier and easier and easier and easier. It's not going to bring more people on the mat; it's not."

"There's no doubt that in the dōjō situation a system of promotions works. Why? This is because the teacher, the person in charge, is actually in charge. Well, unless we're talking about a b.s. dōjō. The problem arises when you move from the dōjō or the small organization situation to the larger organization: then the commercial logic takes over because they have to compete. It's the usual story; they need to have structures on the ground. It's hard to advertise yourself saying: 'We're brilliant but our teachers are only third dan', while the other guy next door is sixth."

"So, no, no, wait. Believe me, I'm living in a place where if you take the test and you pass the test, whatever it is for, like the *gao-kao*[5]; the test to go to university, then you're in, right? You've got the certificate. Must be true. That's a foundational aspect of the culture. From that culture this mindset was spread to Korea and into Japan and, you know, they have a cultural debt to the origination of that system. You might be a complete idiot but you are what the test says you are. And we know not all 'dan' grades are alike. The other question though is, if it's a non-competitive martial art, do you need it at all? I would say that on the one hand yes; you do, because I think the hierarchy has benefits in and of itself. I think that the notion of milestones in practice is good for students. Ideally, in some kind of purist kind of way, no, we don't need it. Let's all train for the sake of training but I think it has enough benefit that it's worthwhile. How do you sort out the problem? I'm not sure. And what you said is completely accurate. When you expand it to the bigger group, you end up running into money. And then you run into empire building. You know, people, teachers get competitive and they want to grow their slice of the pie. It's important to be able to say 'no'.

"You know, what's going on right now in China with me, for example. I just had two different cities contact me again about joining us. One of the gents, however, is just talking too much

---

[5] 高考; gāokǎo; 'Higher Education Exam', is a standardized college entrance exam given annually in mainland China.

about money, so I'll probably end up saying... [Laughs.] I've lived in Asia for a long time. My wife, Korean-American, would say to me: 'You can't talk to white people anymore; they don't understand you; you're too indirect'. So, I'll say no like they do in Asia: 'Ah, you know, I'm just not the right person to help you realize your dreams', or 'I don't think I could support you properly", rather than what I would say if I was just using the old Yankee Doodle kind of way of talking. Or my Scottish way of talking. Might be different. [Both laughing] That's just me again; it gets back to the book. That's my Way. You do whatever you want.

"The thing that's funny in terms of worrying about what other people are doing? If this experience, life, that you're going through right now, is just a bunch of electronic bleeps and bloops and charges, in a carbon-based life form? It's some massive accident? Then what the hell does matter? It's just one accidental monkey telling another accidental monkey what he thinks about a monkey's ideas that they made up. Doesn't make any difference; right? Justice! Or this or that? I mean; who cares? It's meaningless. The world's going to drift away as a snowball one day when the sun burns out.

"If it means something more than that? Then, you know - and I'm not saying what that something more is - well, then maybe these ideals, these notions and ideas, are important. I don't have the answer. I've just done what I've done; okay? And, then again, I've had many compromises. I think Furuya sensei is up in the sky some place laughing at me, because I see how it happens – the slip in standards."

"I suppose the only thing we can do individually is to do things with integrity. That's all and it doesn't matter if other people do differently, as you say. In the end, it doesn't really change anything".

*William Gillespie*

# Searching for Aikidō Applied

"Fundamentally, many people training have no idea of what they're doing and what they're doing it for. A lot of the problems that we were experiencing as a community are probably due - among other things - to the fact that our objectives are not really that well defined. As a consequence, it is difficult to deal with any issues we are confronted with."

"When a Japanese asks me: 'What dan are you William?', I say: '*Joudan*', '*Ouki joudan*', which means 'I'm a big joke'. [Both Laughing] Anyway, it's an experience. The other day at Hombu, I was practicing with a middle-aged lady and, after class, she's talking to my friend. My friend has quite good Japanese and she's like: 'Oh my god. I couldn't move him' and he looks at her and points at me: 'This guy's *rokudan*, shihan. How are you going to move him?' I don't think people know what they're doing in class. I shouldn't say that out loud. Waiting for the hate mail! [Laughing] People don't realize what they're doing and some of the criticism of Aikidō as being... we'll get to that too... is valid, you know, I'm not sure people fully understand what they're actually doing in their training. This idea of moving people and whether or not it worked or not?"

"In a time when Aikidō practice is getting, we could say, watered down to make it more accessible, and when the community in its entirety is criticized because we're not dealing well with other styles, you actually have experiences that go exactly in the opposite direction. You taught Aikidō in MMA schools, you have exchange experiences with Brazilian Jiujitsu teachers. I had a good look at your YouTube channel, Aikidō Applied. If you're curious, people, go and have a look. What you propose is quite at odds with the recent tendency to soften art. So my next question is this: in your opinion, does traditional Aikidō include all that is necessary to fulfill its objectives as a Budō? We also can discuss what Aikidō is today, if it's still a Budō or not. Does Aikidō need to be evolved? Because in the meantime a lot of things have happened. New combat sports, MMA have emerged. What's your take on this? Tradition or innovation?"

"Well, I think that, fundamentally, people need to understand what Aikidō is at the start and, I think, [Laughing] that somebody's made an entire internet presence on being really bad at Aikidō (unknown to him) and having misconceptions about it from the start. It's quite funny; I mean, seeing someone, whether they realize it or not, trying to say Aikidō is bad, when they're lousy, and then making an entertainment channel out of it, complaining that all of Aikidō is fake? It's a bit 'interesting'. People have misconceptions about what Aikidō is at the start. I think that principally, you know... O-sensei's looking at it, from what I've read and discussions with people and meeting teachers who were students of his. [Pauses.] What is Aikido? One thing that people forget about Kisshomaru sensei and O-sensei is that he's his son. It's not like they're not having conversations about Aikidō right? It's not like O-sensei's going to fail to say 'Hey', you know, they're having breakfast, they have the *natto* and the rice or whatever and the pickles, you know, 'what you were doing was total nonsense'. You know what I mean? [Both laughing] Blood is thicker than water and people forget this, which is amazing. I just think that people... they get frustrated immediately. What is Aikido training in the main? What can Aikido be in the hands of some? As far as application, I look at Aikidō like the piano or maybe it's even more complex, maybe it's the pipe organ where you have to use your hands, you have to use your bloody feet, right? And then pull levers and all kinds of things. It's a very complicated, in a good way, and technical instrument.

"Aikidō is like this as a martial art, if you seek utility beyond the core benefits: body, mind and spirit. Applied technique requires deep development. For example, people use the term 'internal strength', but let's say other parts of the body other than your major muscle groups (which have to be developed too). It requires the strengthening of your fascia, your tendons, your ligaments in a unique way. It involves learning how to expand and extend your musculoskeletal system at the right moment. How to improve your joint mobility. And then, the coordination of movement with breath to maximize power. That's a long process.

"Getting back to what Aikidō was, what it is, you know, we use the word 'Aikidō' like it is some monolithic thing, but it's a giant tent and then inside that tent are all these different expressions of it. It's like what we talked about, the mat at Hombu Dōjō, where you have all these different people doing different things in the same space. I wrote about that in the book. They're all doing 'Aikidō' on the mat at the same time. I use the analogy that it's like surfing. I can take you to Waikiki and it's really easy and you've got a 12 foot board and away you go, right? But I can take you to Mavericks in Half Moon Bay and not only will the massive waves kill you but the sharks will eat you too. It's different. It's all surfing but it's not quite the same experience.

"The mistake people make ... the first misstep they make is 'what is Aikidō?'. I personally think it is, as intensively as you can bear, the drilling of martial arts techniques to develop you as a human being: body, mind and spirit. From what I can gather, that is his original broad intention of the art. Developing better humans.

"And yet, it still has this *ouyouwaza*, 応用技, applied technique, issue because that seems to be an aim as well. This idea of 'making it work' or 'getting it right'. Now, I think there's merit in pursuing this kind of functionality in practice because it makes you aim for a result, even if in a narrow context, and makes you aim for a kind of perfection. Otherwise, it's just what I call *Aiki-undo*, just exercise, like calisthenics, one-two-three-four, right? Actually, I often say there are three types of Aikidō practice: *Aiki-Budō* (and that's getting smaller), then you have Aiki-undo (aiki-exercise), which is just people practicing fast and throwing each other cooperatively and jumping around, and then you've got Aiki-cosplay, which is sort of like a philosophy lesson in Japanese clothes, then you go out for beers. That'll get me in trouble.

"So anyway, you have this first issue: what is it? The definition of it can still include the subset of ouyouwaza. I think that people have not investigated... Number one, most of them that are trying to apply it, have not grounded themselves sufficiently in the fundamentals. Number two, they haven't developed a proper aiki-body - one that's more like a coiled snake rather than just rigid iron. I know a lot of guys that do a lot of weapons, but when I look at them doing Aikidō, I think '*ude-bakari*' - just with their arms. Especially in the West, where people's upper-bodies can be built very powerfully, there's a tendency to just want to push. I see Francesco's picture up here on your list of videos. I showed him today something about how he's using his shoulder rather than generating power from the feet, from the floor up.

"So again, we return to this cultural issue of, okay, 'It's got to be black and white', 'It's got to be this way or that way', 'It's got to be on or off', it's binary thinking - the tiny prison of binary ideas. So, you know, it is all these things at the same time. There are lots of different expressions of what Aikidō is. People that are doing Aikidō just as cosplay or pseudo-psychology, a sort of 'happy clappy Aikidō', they love it! Let them go do it. That's great! What's their ability to defend themselves? Now, when I ask that, you've got to divide it into two parts. One is match fighting and sports fighting. I cover this in the book in the chapter called *'Aikidō Keiko in an MMA World'* and then again in *'Wrestling with Aikidō'*, which isn't wrestling with Aikidō in a literal sense but struggling mentally with Aikidō. Second is the self-defense paradigm.

"For the match fighting paradigm, can you take Aikidō techniques and could you use Aikidō as a base upon which to then go participate in the sport of MMA? Of course. Is that the highest or best use of O-sensei's Art of Peace? Probably not, but maybe we need someone to do it. You see Aikidō techniques in MMA. For sure; you see people do it. And I predicted, in my book, that ultimately people would try to mine it for things that they could add to the MMA 'game'. And I would say that people also don't study deeply enough when it comes to application. Okay? So let's say we have this main thing that everybody's doing and that's developing yourself as a human being through the rigorous drilling of martial arts techniques of Aikidō and that's great. What a wonderful thing to do for all of society, for humanity. And, I get it; there's no contest in Aikidō but then at the same time can I take that base and use it if I have a real confrontation? I, unfortunately, have had actual confrontations before and, like you said, I've taught in different contexts. I have witnesses that have seen them so it's not like I'm spinning a story. Yeah: of course you can. I think that you start by building fundamentals, but fundamentals are 'boring'. People get bored with that and they want to go on to something else, especially now with the mentality of an iPhone and an app and 'I can google it' and I can do whatever I like because I make my own reality. Then you watch a YouTube video of Aikidō and you can't feel it. You can't see the power of this person, you don't know what it's like. I've had people the first time they grab my wrist or you know people they grab you and you expand your wrist with *kokyu*, with your breath, and you know how to use all the meat in your body, not just the major muscles and people freak out. They go: 'What the hell?'. 'What's that?'

"And maybe there's a marketing issue in that and I think that I said this in the book; I mean, you know it's like Elvis Costello: 'What's so funny about peace, love and understanding?'. I think the world is full of nihilistic jerks and narcissists these days. Unfortunately. We all have that internal struggle and you should direct yourself away from that. That's a very unfulfilling existence. You should pull your mind away from these things. Concentrate on things that are beautiful and inspiring and helpful and constructive. You're going to live a lot better, more satisfying life if you do that instead of constantly tearing things apart all the time and doubting everything.

"So do I think that you can add things to Aikidō? Sure. Does it help? Have I cross-trained? Yeah; did it help me? Sure. Did I try to go use Aikidō on them? No. I just did what they did. I just did what they did to learn what they did. I liked being a beginner again; I liked that a lot. I did *newaza*; I liked the experience of pressure from someone on top of you. Can you apply principles? Sure: eventually; sure. Did it improve my ukemi? Yeah; it did. One thing, nobody at the MMA academies laughed at my Aikidō class. A lot of people said:

'That looks too dangerous. I don't want to do that. I don't like it. I don't want to get slammed on the ground like that'.

"However, I think we can't lose sight of this bigger thing that Aikidō is and this bigger objective of its contribution to culture and human conflict. It still is that, so it's again people dealing with these dichotomies, they just want it to be resolved. They want it to be all one way or all the other way."

"Or they just want to make noise?"

"Well, there's that too. Like I said, 'What's so funny about peace, love and understanding?' There are people that don't like it and there are forces in the world that don't like O-sensei's message. They don't like it at all. And that message is also running counter to human nature. I was raised a Calvinist and 'People are no damn good', to just simplify John Calvin. [Laughing] There: now you don't read his books. He also identifies that people have great capacity to do good. I think Aikidō in a way, just the typical *kata-keiko*, has a way of developing that in human beings. As a real martial artist you should develop compassion as well. It's nice to be strong but you need to develop other things. I mean, in all Japanese martial arts you've got *tai-iku* - developing your body. You've got developing your mind - *chi-iku* and you've got *ki-iku* – developing your energy. Then there is *toku-iku* – developing your ethics. I think Aikidō is particularly good at that - the ethics of not destroying.

"And then there is cultivating *jyoshiki no kanryo*, which is common sense – doing the right act, in the right way, at the right moment. Like if I'm on the mat and it's the middle of class and I point in an area that has two things and say: 'Hand me that' and there's a banana and there's a *tanto* (knife). I probably don't want the banana but if it's after class and people are having a drink on the mat (they shouldn't but they are) and I say hand me that – maybe I want to eat the banana. And finally there is *kan* or *choukan* which it's interesting. The Chinese call it *di-liu-gan* which means sixth feeling (sense) but actually I think the Japanese word, the way they look at it, is perception, your ability to perceive something fully, deeply.

"Now, I never learned any of that in the competitive martial arts I've done or dabbled in and, you know, Aikidō has a message of human development which should be principal and primary. Then, after that, we do need to develop some people a bit *mooki-mooki* (muscular) who have some vim and vigor. I think that's important. But not everybody has to do that and it's okay not to do it! It's okay not to be able to do it! It's okay, if you're not Michael Jordan and you still love basketball. It's okay if you go to an eighth grader's game and it's all played below the rim. It's still basketball. I don't know if any of this makes any sense but I think that my stance has been, as you noticed from my channel, I'm not trying to add things to it. Like saying, I've got to add boxing. It may help me because... [Stops]

"Here's the thing. For example, *shomenuchi*, I had someone say to me the other night: 'Oh, that's completely useless'. I said: 'Listen. I have a friend in Beijing who is doing BJJ with me. Big kid, from Texas, had been a baseball pitcher at Texas A&M University. So he's a first division collegiate athlete in the USA. I knew many at UCLA and God, in making them, just went 'shazam!' and they're amazing physical specimens. This guy goes to a bike parking lot at the subway station in Beijing and gets into an altercation with the local guy running the bike lot. That local fellow had probably had a hard day, too many drinks and a bad argument with his wife. They exchange words. Guy goes into the shed and comes out a hammer and starts swinging at my friend. He's playing for keeps. My friend has done Muay Thai and BJJ. Hammer hit him several times; I think it broke his hand and arm. Classic untrained 'defensive' wounds from a weapon. Eventually, he bested the guy - barely - but my friend was very lucky he didn't end up hit in a worse place, in hospital or jail (for striking a local) or all three.

"So there you go. There's the typical movement that someone's using at a very simple level. It's a movement that we train with all the time. Yeah; there's much more complex ways to hold weapons and hit but as a fundamental pedagogical starting point shomenuchi is a wonderful way to instill principles. It's a way to develop the *nage*. It's a way to develop uke. It is a way to understand *ma-ai* (spacing/timing) principles, understand lines of attack and angles of deflection - that you've honed with weapons particularly - and you apply that to different sorts of striking. It's not that complicated, but nobody's doing it. I mean some people are doing it; that's not fair. I know some people are doing it and probably doing it better than me but, in Beijing, it was just this experiment I had initiated. Unfortunately it got derailed a bit because of Covid. I'll get back to making proper content. Japan's been a pretty soft lockdown but I have uke available to me here and we're going to start, I think, a small class here - a kind of a study group at a dōjō. If I tell you how here, then you won't watch the channel!

"So these are things that people can do after class or as a special class to add on to the main Aikidō they know. When someone says 'I do Aikidō' to me, that's like someone saying, 'I'm a Christian' or 'I'm a Jew' or a Muslim. It could mean many things within a certain context. It's a big tent. Within the word are all kinds of different expressions of it. Look, if you want to learn newaza, go study a newaza system. If you want to study the spacing and timing of a striking system just go study that system a little bit. You don't have to do that system's techniques to adapt to it. You can adapt to other things because it's really all the same after a while. A strike, a kick, a grab, it all becomes very similar.

"One of the great things about Aikidō training is developing the "Aiki body". I have a lot of friends that have done, for example, a lot of newaza but their back is overdeveloped. You know; their lats. They spend so much time on the ground, on their backs, that they develop this scallop shape and don't really move well on their feet. Aikidō develops you in a well-rounded way – left and right side - and it is a great base for then learning other martial arts. It is a tremendous thing. And ukemi, right? It is not just capitulation. At its lowest level, it's capitulation. Chiba sensei has written a great piece about it being the art of recovery or the art of survival. You can find it on the internet. I was lucky to be able to be in his dōjō in London for a while and met a lot of great people there and still have a great *senpai* up north, Mike Flynn sensei, in Scotland. Check him out.

"I think that ukemi is something that people don't fully understand. When you're practicing with someone... [Pauses] It's like me the other night at Hombu. I practiced with this middle aged lady. What was I going to do? Just grab her and lock her up or hit her so hard I break her arm? This is ridiculous. I just gave her enough of a feeling and pressure that she can train and make it a little difficult for her. She may misunderstand it, frankly. She may think, mistakenly, that I'm resisting her, because it's more difficult to move me than someone else but I'm actually doing her a favor. I'm actually helping her. I'm not just doing the typical pretty easy capitulation. I wrote a note to my students in China recently about this, about how the lowest level of Aikidō is just this sort of capitulation as uke. I know someone that got injured recently because he thought the teacher was going to do a technique and then you know he zigged when the teacher zagged and basically he jumped when he shouldn't have and now he's buggered his shoulder. That's really his mistake. I think maybe I am going in the other direction; I tend not to run with the herd so much you know. I question people disregarding things they don't fully understand. I see people questioning training methodology when they don't understand its purpose. You hear the word 'evolve'. [Laughs.] Okay; now you got to a pet peeve. To me 'evolve' is shorthand for 'Hey man; don't make me do anything that I really don't want to do'. Just let me do what I like. That's it; yeah; I think that's pretty much it. You know, the great John Wooden said that 'To progress you must change but not all change is progress'. Know why? Not for some whim."

*William Gillespie*

*Hiroshi Tada*

# The Aiki-body

"William, you already mentioned the Aiki-body and the way you developed it. Currently, there's a new definition to indicate that, 'internal power training', even though this sort of internal training has actually been out there for quite some time. We have historic sensei, like Koichi Tohei or Hiroshi Tada, who have developed internal power training systems since the 70s. What about the Aikikai Hombu Dōjō? Is this still not really a matter for discussion, or not openly anyways?"

"Yes. I think the focus there is on more basic fundamentals but you can feel it in some people. I would say that some *keiko* are more disposed to being utilized by you to work on some of those concepts. It's always available but I think it's in some classes because of the way they're structured or the teacher's *waza* or the teacher's focus makes it a little easier to work on. Again, it's not spoken of overtly and again we struggle with the idea 'Hey, it's not up front, man. How come you haven't mechanized the whole thing for me?', 'How come it's not systematized?', 'Why don't I have an app?'. You see what I mean? Again, we run into this sort of cultural issue. However, if I make it so straightforward? How do you develop *jyoshiki no kanryo*? *Kan* or *choukan*?

"I'd say that Hombu Dōjō is 'bowling', if you want a cricket reference, but nobody understands cricket so let's stick with baseball. I lived next to Lords Cricket Grounds and I still don't get it. So Hombu is 'pitching down the middle', about 70 miles or 80 miles an hour. You're not being thrown fastballs. So it's being pitched at a speed for the broadest audience possible to hit. Sorry; I started talking about these things but I interrupted you before you even finished your question, which is a lawyer's habit."

"Well I was interested in knowing if you actually have some kind of training regime in that sense?"

"Yes; I do. You can see small aspects of it in two videos I posted on Aikidō Applied. I do some of my physical and breathing training. It's not all of it by any stretch and it's not done in the order that I do it. This is an interesting question because I've been lucky in a couple ways again. Unlucky in plenty of ways too. If you have some time after this we could go on about that for a while and have a couple drinks but I've been lucky at Aikidō in a number of ways, like being in Los Angeles, getting to go to Japan, meeting some great senpai in Japan, cultivating a senpai in the UK, etc.

"About 15 years ago, maybe more, I started to experience my own Aikidō in a way where I started to understand how I was generating power and where I was generating power from. I became much more conscious about this and then I became interested in sports medicine. If I could do university over again at U.C.L.A. I'd have been an East Asian studies major and Kinesiology major. Youth is wasted on the young. So, I started to study the fascia system and then I had some other experiences in training. In newaza, an Aikikai shihan friend of mine held me down in Beijing. *Yoko-shiho-gatame*, side control, and he only weighs maybe 60 kilos? My God; the guy felt like he was 500 kilos. Phenomenal. How?

*Arnold Schwarzenegger and Kensho Furuya*

"I had this awakening from what I was experiencing in my training and began examining it. How do you study martial arts? It's *Gakku, Jiutsu, Dou*. Right? It's Study, Technique, Way - the three pillars of studying any martial art. So I am figuring out a few things on my own and then, all of a sudden, I meet another martial artist and we kind of become friends; you know, older guy who has been doing Aikidō and *Kobudō* for a long time, and we just hit it off. He has been articulating for me some of the experiences and discoveries I have made through training. Ultimately, all martial arts are experiential; they're not conceptual. I can talk about it all day long and you're not going to understand it, right? How big was the wave? It was so big it was going to kill me! Wow! I was walking on the moon. Oh, it was great, you know. You had to be there. You have to experience it, but my friend has been able to articulate to some extent, a glimpse, to point in the right direction for me. 'Look; this is what you're experiencing' and 'this is where you can take it to a next level'. I showed Francesco a few things today about how I use the *jo* or *bokken*. I don't get caught up in this or that *kata*; it's a tool for me to develop my body, that's it, and to understand principles. Kata are helpful for that sometimes, but I have solo training I do with weapons. I have solo training I do with other devices like a kind of long staff that's imbalanced and difficult to manipulate. And I have been experimenting with weights in unconventional ways.

"One of the interesting things about Furuya sensei was that before he became obese he was actually quite fit like a 28 inch waist and a 44 coat. He was like a V. He used to go down and lift at Venice Beach and he knew Schwarzenegger and he told me the most amazing thing about that guy. He said: 'I'm going to be Mr. Universe' and he became Mr. Universe. And then he went: 'I'm going to be a movie star' and did it. And then: 'I'm going to go into politics'. Darn if he didn't do them all. The copious notes Furuya sensei has on his weightlifting experiences is something I covet. Come on David Ito! Cough it up! [Laughs] David has the notes: what he used, what he thought about it, how it worked and how it didn't work. Years back, I started experimenting with sort of weights and medicine balls and kettlebells not always in the conventional ways that people are using them; and then isometric exercises and my own body weight exercises and then coordinating that with breath and then taking those ideas and principles and trying to employ them on the mat. That's really what I'm doing all the time in the classes in Hombu Dōjō now. That's all I really do. I'm not interested in some kind of fast aerobics class or, I mean, I'll do it if I have to but the idea of going there and pounding people like I used to when I was younger, it just seems ridiculous. As I said to you earlier, it can't be the other guy's fault all 5,452 times. Maybe I'm the problem. I'm trying to train a bit smarter and, to answer your question, definitely. It is a personal exploration. I don't understand the concept of *Ki*. Not yet; I'm kind of exploring that in my own sort of infant way. I find it fascinating because it's a way of now trying to take my Aikidō to a new level.

"I think too of living my own life and how to try to improve that as well. This notion of self-cultivation is part of what appealed to me about East Asian culture. This idea of Way to develop myself as a human being. It turns life into kind of a game, in a way, or art. You know; the notion of trying to make your life a work of art. Unfortunately, in my work of art I've spilled a lot of paint. It's finger painting; it's not always the best picture, but it's mine. I own it. [Laughing]

"To answer your question, I do have a regimen. I could tell you but then I'd have to kill you and all the people reading the book. I don't feel I'm in a position to teach the ideas. It's interesting though, I did teach, I have a buddy that teaches at the British school here and he asked me to come in and teach some playground Aikidō to his group. I just showed them simple things. The kids loved it - really young kids and then older teens and adults. I gave them some drills and things. I would show them: 'Look can you feel this? Now all my power is coming from my shoulder' and 'From my skeleton now', 'Can you feel this? It's all coming from the floor and my feet pushing into the floor'; and then me sort of wringing my whole body like you'd wring a towel. Breath power is real: why are they exhaling? Why are they making a noise? Why are they doing it, you know, if this was nonsense? It wouldn't add anything. In weight lifting, however, it's the same thing."

"Jimmy Connor[5]."

"Well, there's that. True. It's a new area that I've experienced in my practice and was kind of: 'Hey, what's that all about? Oh, this is interesting'. And then I began to use it in my own solo training. Now I'm trying to more formalize how I'm studying it with people that know more and have gone farther than I have and, you know, they're helping me.

"Ultimately you've got to do it yourself though, right? You have to experience it on your own. I can sit there and tell you how to surf all day long but ultimately you've got to experience it yourself and so that's what I'm trying to do. I think that kind of training takes a real steady commitment. We were talking about O-sensei, in the past, and who's going to be doing what he did? I mean he starts off as youth training in swimming, then it's *sumo* and imbibing Japanese culture and then he was so passionate about politics. Then you've got farming and homesteading and Judō and then all the kobudō he did and the weapons and the army and going overseas. Can you create that same kind of experience? And don't forget

---

[5] Famous professional tennis player who did a kind of kiai every time he struck a ball in a match.

*Daito-ryu Jiujitsu* and then *Shingon* Buddhism, esoteric Buddhism, and then his *misogi* which involves all kinds of really austere practices. I mean who's really doing that? There's a good book on that that Ellis Amdur has written. I have ripped off all the ideas and I've told everybody here as if it's my own. [Laughing then whispering] Don't tell him: he's a large human being." [Both laughing]

*Morihei Ueshiba*

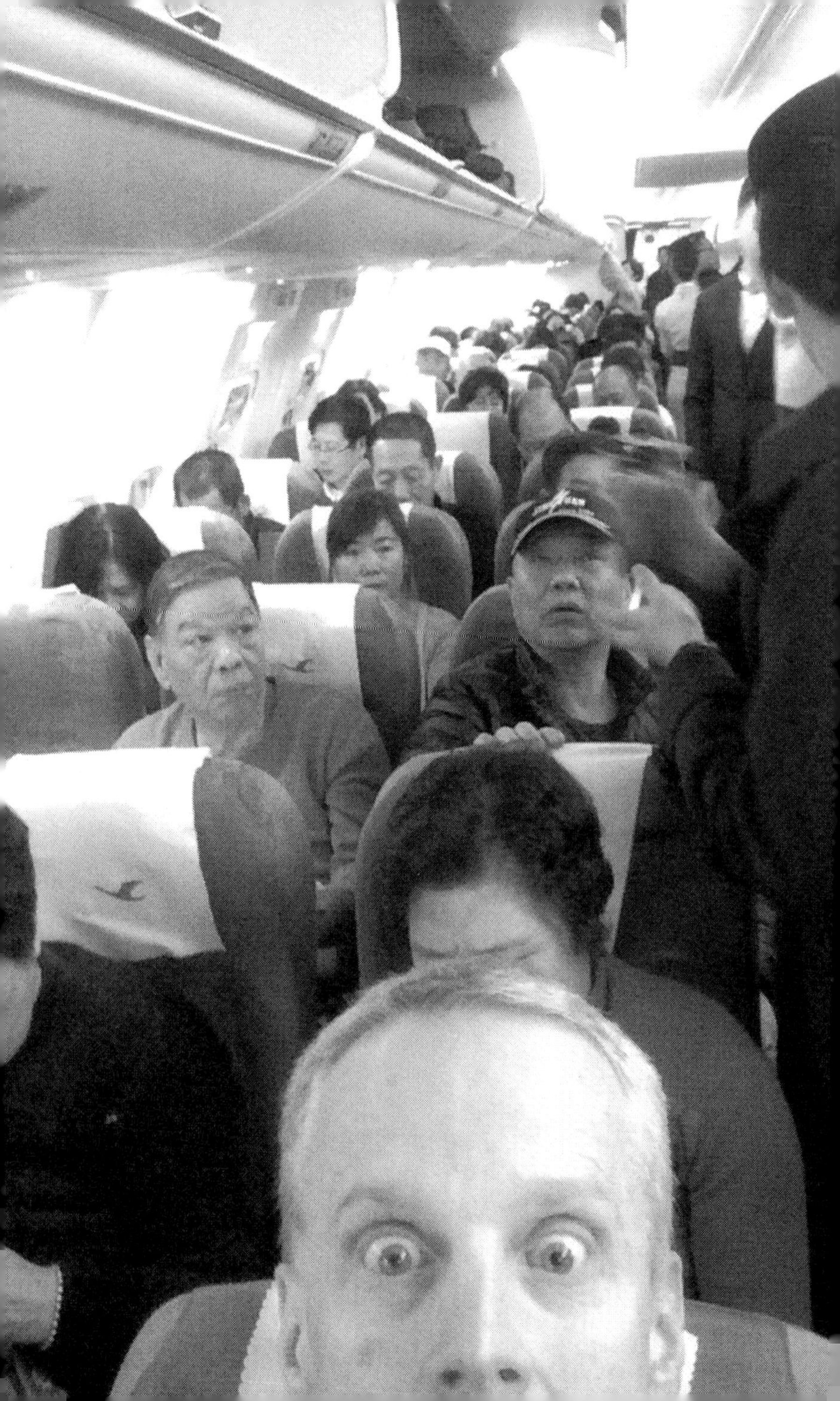

# Being an Aikidō Pioneer in China

"Throughout our conversation, you mentioned more times how China and your Chinese experience have been a major turning point in your life. You've been there for a while: you took it upon yourself to bring a Japanese martial art to China."

"Good Lord. What was I thinking? How do you say crazy in Italian?"

"*Matto!*"

"Matto! Maybe *stupido*?"

"I suppose there are a lot of preconceptions about this, because I'm sure Chinese people don't do only Chinese things; it's like if you're Italian you don't only eat pasta, you eat a variety of different foods. Can you tell us a bit about your experience in China? What is it like being an Aikidō teacher in China?"

"Sure. Well, first of all, the people are the best thing about being there. I mean, I love it, I do. I love the people. It's different wherever you go in China. The world's getting more homogenized but, you know, Italy has its regionalism, the US does too, however, because of television and the internet all of that's changing a bit. China is a big place and there are lots of different cities: so different they can't understand each other sometimes. In Beijing I liked the people when I first went there.

"China was sort of the opposite of Japan - instead of endless rules it was *'rules-shmools'*. It's similar but completely different. I went there originally because I had to leave Japan after my wife got very ill. You can read about it in the book. About how if I wasn't doing Budō for years, there's no doubt she would have died. If I had made the wrong decision about going to the hospital or refusing an ambulance to a Yokohama hospital, she'd be dead. For sure.

"Anyway, that happened in 2003, before our daughter was born. Had my wife died then, I probably would be in some bar in Roppongi drunk, if I was still alive. But, she didn't and we ended up getting to London because her health insurance was through Lloyds of London. I had a chance through family contacts to land a good UK job, but I suddenly had this opportunity to work in China, so I grabbed it.

"China was opening up more at the time. Everybody in London was running out to China with their hair on fire and I proposed starting an advisory business in finance with three other guys I knew. It sounds almost like a joke: a Yank, an Englishman from The Rugby School and two Scotsmen walk into a bar. I think that's how the first opium war started? Actually, it was a couple of Scotsman and a battleship, but shush. Anyway, we decided to do this advisory business and we were hunting for deals in China but I added the idea of looking in Korea and Japan, a triangular business model, so I started going out to China – 3 months there, 3 months back

*William Gillespie in China*

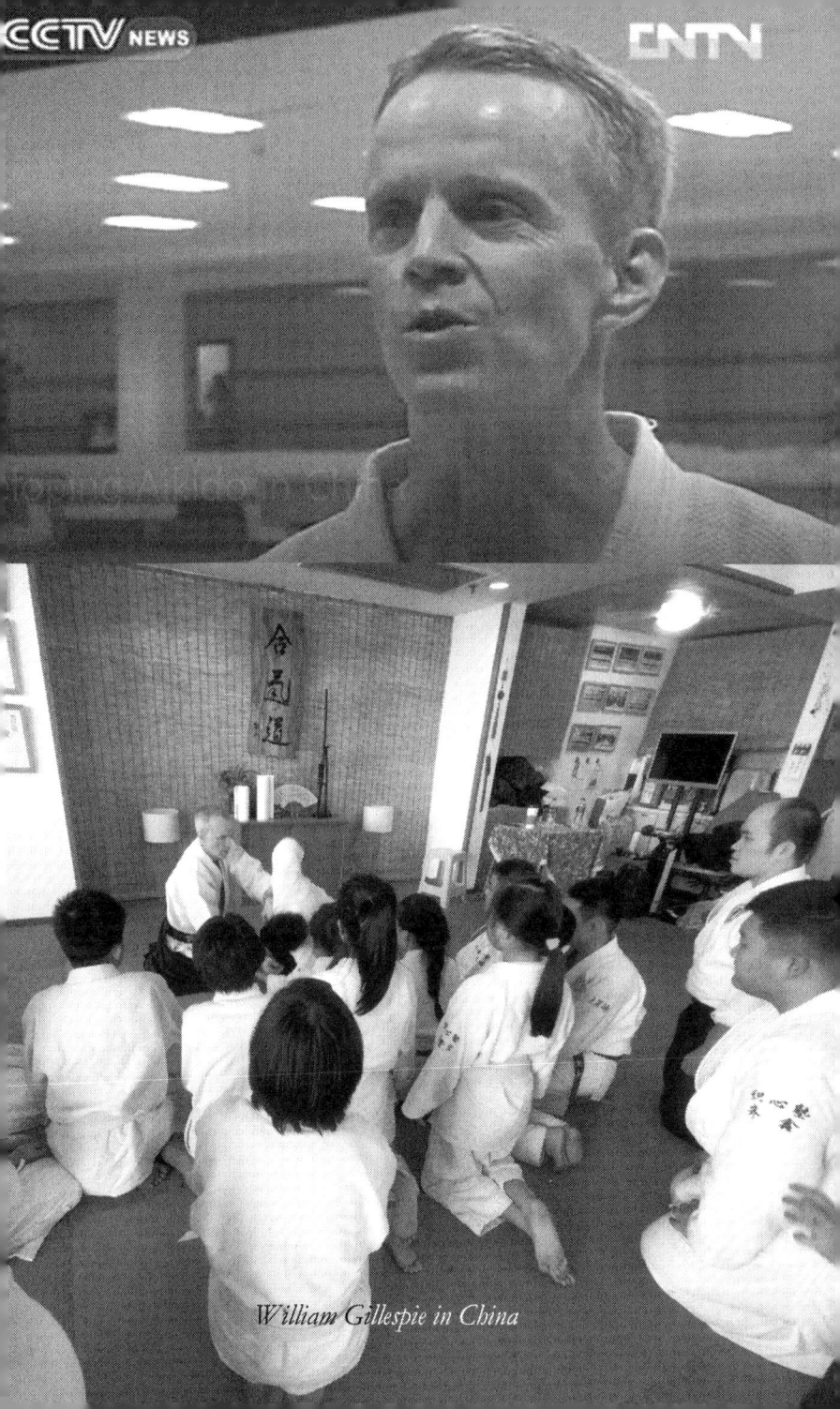

合气会暨北京神流馆合气道应用技法讲

*Moments of Caikikai*

in London. I had been training in Chiba sensei's London dōjō. Eric Beke and Steve Beecham were running it at the time.

"When I went to China, I decided to try Aikidō there, so I went to Suganuma sensei's group at Beijing University. There was just a guy, a student covering the class. Suganuma sensei and Furuya sensei had lived in Hombu Dōjō together so I had extra respect for him. It was great. China was just developing then. It was totally different than it is now. Very different. It was changing and Chinese people were starting to do different things and economically it was improving and they wanted to try different kinds of food and they wanted to try different sports and so Aikidō was one of the things they wanted to try. In Beijing, Aikidō started in 2002. I arrived in 2005. China was booming economically and I saw Beijing transformed - the way it looked before the Olympics and then afterward was amazing.

"Then I was training with a second group there that was under Takase shihan from New Zealand. Closer to our home. A Hombu Dojo shihan, who I knew from Hombu training days, Mori sensei came to Beijing to teach a seminar in 2005. He sees me on the mat and comes over and gives me a big hug. All the Chinese are like: 'Who the hell is this white monkey he's hugging?' Afterwards, some Chinese students asked if I would teach at their dōjō and I said: 'Well, go ask your shihan first. If it's okay, no problem.' Takase sensei was great. He said: 'Sure; have him come', so I was doing that for a while. Then they kept changing locations, which is a Beijing thing. Landlords were fickle tricksters pulling this, pulling that, so you had to move places a lot.

"I got tired of it and then in London I rebooted my BJJ training at Roger Gracie Academy and when in China I was doing BJJ at Gracie China, under two American black belt students of Pedro Sauer, a close student of Rickson Gracie. I didn't tell them I did Aikidō but an American BJJ teacher came up to me one day and said: 'Wait a second. I know you do martial arts because you sit *seiza*, you tie your own belt seiza and you pay attention (unlike the rest of the other students). What traditional martial arts did you do?' I told them and one teacher was crazy about Aikidō; he loved it. We're still friends, Chet Quint. He's a great guy who has done all sorts of martial arts: Taekwondo, Karate, *Shuaijiao*, BJJ, Judō, etc. A former US Army and police officer. Top notch! He's down in Jakarta or Kuala Lumpur nowadays. A really good guy.

"They asked me if I would start lessons at the Muay Thai/BJJ/MMA Academy. I said 'sure' and it was great. It was like Christmas, because I got Thai boxing students and I got BJJ students and MMA students and people that are much more physically capable than your average Aikidō student these days. That's been the biggest trouble with Aikidō of late. It's that the talent pool is so shallow. People like the guy I mentioned, Tony Hind? Now? He'd be doing BJJ or probably be winning MMA fights, not doing Aikidō.

"I was able to swap lessons. BJJ can be a bit expensive, so I was able to trade lessons. Eventually, I started my own dōjō because again the owners (not the teachers) were moving locations. This sort of thing got a bit ridiculous, so I started my own dōjō - Beijing Aikikai. It was growing pretty steadily throughout 2015, 2016, 2017 – though I wasn't running it as a business - and then I started having a few issues. Some local teachers tried to dissuade people from coming to my dōjō. 'He's gonna break your arm. He's gonna hurt you. William's a monster'. God bless them. The problem is that it's easy to try to attract somebody to class with marketing and puffing. But can you develop them? Retain them? That's the really difficult thing to do as a teacher. It doesn't matter what belt someone gives you, if you can't keep people on the mat, if you can't

*William Gillespie takes ukemi for Tsuruzo Miyamoto in Beijing*

develop good students, what does it matter? You're no teacher. Despite the attacks, I just tried to encourage everybody. I was organizing seminars there for Hombu Dōjō from time to time. The same malcontents would try to block others from attending. Eventually, I invited Miyamoto shihan to come. I was the senior person in the community, by far, but I just tried to set a good example and get along. Haters gonna hate. Imagine if they put that energy into training themselves for real!

"In the book, I am playing on people's stereotypes of China and at the end of the chapter on China, I'm like: 'No: Aikidō is just as messed up, has all the problems that Aikidō has everywhere else in the world'. It's just another set of human beings. It's going to have issues but there's a lot of really sincere good people and I love all my students, of course. As people became more comfortable with me, because I'm not Chinese, I don't know if anybody had noticed in the last couple hours, I'm not Chinese. Another spoiler alert! [Laughing] It took people a while to get used to me, especially with the gossips working overtime, and now there is momentum building: 'Hey, you know, he's not trying to control or make money off us'. You have to grow the plant in whatever soil it's planted. I've been lucky. I have had some really good people join me from another city, who are also very dear to me, and then that has grown to other cities.

"I just got contacted again about someone else that wants to join CAikikai (my group of dōjō). This is just my Way. There's a lot of other ways to do Aikidō. It's like we talked about – 'the big tent'. Other people like the way they're doing it, let them do it. My Way will never be very popular because it is too hard. No easy promotions. No easy practice. Real martial arts. Martial arts are egalitarian in that everyone can try them. They are exclusive in that not everyone can do them at a high level.

"However, I tell my students: 'No matter how hard we train, never ever look down on anybody else and their Aikidō'. What they're doing, they like doing. A kind of superior attitude just eats away at you like a cancer, so don't think of yourself as better; you're just doing what you enjoy and what you like the way you want to express it.

"As far as martial arts go, you know, Chinese aren't typically as aggressive physically as maybe your average westerner. The notion of competitive sports was a relatively new thing there. They've certainly excelled at it in the Olympics, for example. Of course, they have their own martial traditions like *Shuaijiao* (Chinese wrestling) which is quite formidable and then various forms of *gongfu* and you'd see people practicing in the parks. That's going through its own development issues. I don't know the guy that was going around picking fights with *tai chi* 'masters' but I have friends who do. MMA and BJJ and boxing have become a little bit more popular. There is *Sanda*, which is a fighting version of Chinese Wushu but that's not going to appeal to that much of the society, that much of the population. Not a whole lot of women doing it. There's a lot there, if you can find the right teacher. There are great things to learn in Chinese martial arts, e.g., the weaponry is very interesting. There are tremendous things you can learn. Unfortunately, I haven't had a chance to go to Shaolin, which I heard has been rather commercialized. I wanted to go to Wudang mountain, Wudangshan, the birthplace of tai chi. That's still potentially interesting.

"I'm not living there right now, though I still have my dōjō and our flat in Beijing. Due to Covid and other plans, I'm living in Tokyo but the idea has been that my family would move to Tokyo for my daughter's schooling, give my wife a different place to live for a bit and me a chance to learn from some of the Hombu teachers, particularly Miyamoto shihan, because they are getting older. I still want to learn and absorb as much as I can. I thought I'd go back to doing what I was doing originally in China, i.e., living in two places. We were living in London and Beijing from 2005 to autumn 2014 and then principally in China but I'd be three months in, three months out or four months in, two months out. That broke it up nicely. I'd get bored in London and then, you know, head off to China. When in China the pollution and things can also become tiring.

"So we thought we were coming to Japan and then you all know what happened. The virus became an issue on the 23rd of January and our family had a lot of personal loss from all of that but we are going forward as best we can. We went back to the States, California mostly, for about nine months which was again good for me because I got to see people I hadn't seen in years and kind of figure out what, where and how we want to go on in this unstable world. Was it back to London? Was it in the States? The people's republic of California? Or did I want to go back to Japan, as planned? I decided we'd go back to Japan.

"Ultimately, I hope that the world will settle down, when we realize that while this is a challenge it isn't the only or worst virus ever created in the history of humankind. We've been living with these and other bugs for ages. And we can get back to traveling. We still have our flat in Beijing and hope we can go back and sort all that out at some point but we're coping and the dōjō are going fine and I guide them long distance through classes, articles and study sessions. Things are moving ahead, as best we can, as everyone's doing. Everyone had more pressing issues on their plate than whether or not they were practicing. Around the globe, some people haven't been able to practice. In China, practice is back on; people don't wear masks. Even children's classes are on. At Hombu Dōjō, they're wearing face masks."

"The approach worldwide is very different. Over here, indoor training is not allowed. You're still only allowed to train outdoors and even at that, it comes and goes. We really need to wait and see what happens and try to do the best we can with it."

"Yeah. The notion of one size fits all 'global' solutions or, in some cases, even national solutions is an inflexible approach to a complex problem. Even in the United States, you have states that are totally open and some locked down. We have a federalist system, so states are entitled to differ. The rights of the federal government are limited to those granted by the states, though many forget that from time to time. The U.S.A. is a creation of the individual states ceding certain limited powers. Apart from that, the individual states are able to take whatever approach they want. If citizens like a state, you can move there; dislike its management, leave. Just like guys playing in the NBA or the NFL will often sign with teams in Florida or Texas because there's no state income tax. I like a flexible system like that. Let people do what they want. Let them have personal responsibility and personal agency in their lives, just like we do on the mats.

"Aikidō should be building stronger, more adaptable human beings, that's what it should really be doing. It shouldn't be developing weaker and weaker and more offended, bothered people. It should make us more resilient people so that less and less things in life unbalance us."

"I absolutely agree. This has been very very interesting and I hope that the people reading our words will find them useful. Thanks a million for this dialogue, for sharing your experiences and insights with us, William."

"Well, yeah; I'm not special but some of my experiences are different and if that can help people by sharing them, that's great. And, I really want to thank you for the service you're doing to the Aikidō community, you know, and others that do likewise with these kinds of you know forums and exchanges. It's an important thing to do and it's a selfless thing."

"It's quite a complicated time but let's try and stay positive because we're budōka. Our path doesn't change, right? This is what Budō is for, otherwise we wouldn't be training..."

"Yeah, *amor fati*! Shout out to little Isla who put up with me talking in the other room so loudly; she's got to go to bed now.

"Anyway, blessings everyone. Take care."

*William Gillespie with Doshu Moriteru Ueshiba*

# Acknowledgments

I wish to thank William T. Gillespie for authorising the publication of "The Traveler - Find Your Way" and for the long nights he spent revising it. My thanks also go to William for offering me the opportunity to utilise his images, both from his private photo collection and his social media pages. William T. Gillespie has produced a very stimulating book on his personal travel in Aikido, "Aikido and the Way Less Traveled", that you can buy on Amazon[6]. I also recommend you have a good look at his work browsing his YouTube channel "Aikido Applied"[7].

Most of Kensho Furuya's photos have been taken from the Facebook Page "Reverend Kensho Furuya". We are extremely grateful for the beautiful images. [8]

Thanks to Francesco Re, my special agent in Tokyo, who has introduced me to William and several other interesting people.

I would also like to acknowledge Lorena Chierchini for timely and thoroughly proofreading "The Traveler - Find Your Way".

---

[6] https://www.amazon.com/Aikido-Japan-Way-Less-Traveled/dp/0615950140
[7] https://www.youtube.com/c/AikidoApplied
[8] https://www.facebook.com/kensho.furuya

# The Aiki Dialogues

1. The Phenomenologist - Interview with Ellis Amdur
2. The Translator - Interview with Christopher Li
3. The Wrestler - Interview with Rionne "Fujiwara" McAvoy
4. The Traveler - "Find Your Way" - Interview with William T. Gillespie

**Simone Chierchini: The Phenomenologist - Interview with Ellis Amdur**
The Aiki Dialogues - N. 1
Publisher: Aikido Italia Network Publishing
www.aikidoitalianetworkpublishing.com

Ellis Amdur is a renowned martial arts researcher, a teacher in two different surviving Koryū and a former Aikidō enthusiast. His books on Aikidō and Budō are considered unique in that he uses his own experiences, often hair-raising or outrageous, as illustrations of the principles about which he writes. His opinions are also backed by solid research and boots-on-the-ground experience.
"The Phenomenologist" is no exception to that.

**Simone Chierchini: The Translator - Interview with Christopher Li**
The Aiki Dialogues - N. 2
Publisher: Aikido Italia Network Publishing
www.aikidoitalianetworkpublishing.com

Christopher Li is an instructor at the Aikido Sangenkai, a non-profit Aikidō group in Honolulu, Hawaii, on the island of Oahu. He has been training in traditional and modern Japanese martial arts since 1981, with more than twelve years of training while living in Japan. Chris calls himself a "hobbyist with a specialty", however, thanks to his research and writing he has made an important contribution to the understanding of modern Aikidō. His views on Aikidō, its history and future development are unconventional and often "politically incorrect" but he's not afraid to share them.
This is not a book for those unwilling to discuss the official narrative of our art and its people.

**Simone Chierchini: The Wrestler - Interview with Rionne McAvoy**
The Aiki Dialogues - N. 3
Publisher: Aikido Italia Network Publishing
www.aikidoitalianetworkpublishing.com

From Taekwondo wonder kid to Karate State Champion, from Hiroshi Tada Sensei's Gessoji Dōjō to the Aikikai Hombu Dōjō and Yoshiaki Yokota sensei, Rionne "Fujiwara" McAvoy, a star in the toughest professional wrestling league in the world, Japan, has never been one for finding the easy way out.
In "The Wrestler", Rionne McAvoy tells his story in martial arts and explains his strong views on Aikido, physical training and cross-training and reveals where he wants to go with his Aikido.

# I Dialoghi Aiki

1. L'Ermetista - Intervista a Paolo N. Corallini
2. Il Ricercatore - Intervista a Luigi L. Gargiulo
3. Il Filosofo - Intervista ad André Cognard

**Simone Chierchini: L'Ermetista - Intervista a Paolo N. Corallini**
I Dialoghi Aiki - N. 1
Editore: Aikido Italia Network Publishing
www.aikidoitalianetworkpublishing.com

Paolo Nicola Corallini, Iwama Ryu 7° Dan, Aikikai 7° Dan, è il Direttore Tecnico della Takemusu Aikido Association Italy.

Da Iwama e l'incontro con Morihiro Saito sensei, al complesso intreccio fra le diverse pedagogie presenti nell'Aikidō, dai ricordi dell'uomo Morihiro Saito al futuro dell'Aikidō, nel corso di questa conversazione Paolo Corallini offre il suo approccio dotto e ricercato al senso di ciò che esiste sotto al livello visibile dell'Aikidō.

**Simone Chierchini: Il Ricercatore - Intervista a Luigi L. Gargiulo**
I Dialoghi Aiki - N. 2
Editore: Aikido Italia Network Publishing
www.aikidoitalianetworkpublishing.com

Luigi L. Gargiulo è un conoscitore e praticante di discipline orientali sin dall'adolescenza. Laureato in Scienze dell'Informazione, studioso e praticante di Buddismo Zen e 7° Dan in Aikido, dal 1978 pratica lo Shiatsu, di cui ha creato uno stile personale, il MI ZAI Shiatsu, che insegna nell'Istituto MI ZAI da lui fondato. Dal 2020 è inoltre membro della Direzione Didattica dell'Aikikai d'Italia La sua è una vita di studio: dall'Aikido allo Shiatsu, dal Kototama al Waraku, la curiosità di Luigi L. Gargiulo è sempre rimasta attiva. Seguiamolo nel suo percorso formativo di ieri, oggi e domani.

**Simone Chierchini: Il Filosofo - Intervista ad André Cognard**
I Dialoghi Aiki - N. 3
Editore: Aikido Italia Network Publishing
www.aikidoitalianetworkpublishing.com

André Cognard è una delle voci contemporanee più autorevoli nell'ambito del Budo internazionale. Al 1973 risale l'incontro con Hirokazu Kobayashi sensei, allievo diretto di O-sensei Morihei Ueshiba. Riceve il grado di 8°dan e alla morte del suo maestro eredita la guida dell'accademia internazionale Kokusai Aikido Kenshukai Kobayashi Hirokazu Ryu – KAKKHR. Insegnante "itinerante", profondo conoscitore del Giappone e delle sue tradizioni, André Cognard porta nei diversi continenti una tecnica: l'Aikido del suo Maestro; un messaggio umano: l'Aikido al servizio di tutti; un messaggio spirituale: l'Aikido che, come l'uomo, si ricongiunge a se stesso quando diventa semplicemente Arte.

Simone Chierchini
## THE SPIRITUALIST

Interview with
GÉRARD BLAIZE

NEXT ISSUE:

The Aiki Dialogues N°5

Simone Chierchini

The Spiritualist

Interview with
Gérard Blaize

Gérard Blaize, the first non-Japanese Aikido expert to receive the rank of 7th dan Aikikai, spent five and a half years in Japan where he studied Aikido at the Hombu Dōjō in Tōkyō following mainly Kisshomaru Ueshiba and Seigo Yamaguchi. In 1975, he met Michio Hikitsuchi, one of the most respected jikishideshi of the founder of Aikido Morihei Ueshiba, and followed his sole guidance until his teacher's death in 2004. Hikitsuchi Sensei was a Shinto priest as well as martial artist and was one of the few amongst O-Sensei's disciples equipped to understand and genuinely interested in the spiritual aspect of what Morihei Ueshiba was teaching. Hikitsuchi's 10th Dan rank was personally awarded to him by O-sensei without the Aikikai Hombu Dōjō knowledge and approval, a sign of how deep their connection was.
Gérard Blaize has inherited and is still carrying the legacy of Hikitsuchi's Spiritual Aikido to this day.

Printed in Great Britain
by Amazon